Finance and Third World Economic Growth

Finance and Third World Economic Growth

A Statement by the
Research and Policy Committee of the
Committee for Economic Development

Westview Press
BOULDER & LONDON

Westview Special Studies in Social, Political, and Economic Development

This Westview softcover edition is printed on acid-free paper and bound in softcovers that carry the highest rating of the National Association of State Textbook Administrators, in consultation with the Association of American Publishers and the Book Manufacturers' Institute.

Published in 1988 in the United States of America by Westview Press, Inc., 5500 Central Avenue, Boulder, Colorado 80301, and in the United Kingdom by Westview Press, Inc., 13 Brunswick Centre, London WC1N 1AF, England

Library of Congress Cataloging-in-Publication Data
Finance and Third World economic growth/a statement by the Research and Policy Committee of the Committee for Economic Development.
p. cm.—(WVSS in social, political, and economic development)
Includes index.
ISBN 0-8133-7610-6
1. Finance—Developing countries. 2. Developing countries—Economic policy. I. Committee for Economic Development. Research and Policy Committee. II. Series: Westview special studies in social, political, and economic development.
HG195.F53 1988
336′.09172′4—dc19 88-26152
CIP

Printed and bound in the United States of America

The paper used in this publication meets the requirements of the American National Standard for Permanence of Paper for Printed Library Materials Z39.48-1984.

10 9 8 7 6 5 4 3 2

Contents

Tables

RESPONSIBILITY FOR CED STATEMENTS ON NATIONAL POLICY

The Committee for Economic Development is an independent research and educational organization of over two hundred business executives and educators. CED is nonprofit, nonpartisan, and nonpolitical. Its purpose is to propose policies that will help to bring about steady economic growth at high employment and reasonably stable prices, increase productivity and living standards, provide greater and more equal opportunity for every citizen, and improve the quality of life for all. A more complete description of CED appears on page 177.

All CED policy recommendations must have the approval of trustees on the Research and Policy Committee. This committee is directed under the bylaws to "initiate studies into the principles of business policy and of public policy which will foster the full contribution by industry and commerce to the attainment and maintenance" of the objectives stated above. The bylaws emphasize that "all research is to be thoroughly objective in character, and the approach in each instance is to be from the standpoint of the general welfare and not from that of any special political or economic group." The committee is aided by a Research Advisory Board of leading social scientists and by a small permanent professional staff.

The Research and Policy Committee does not attempt to pass judgment on any pending specific legislative proposals; its purpose is to urge careful consideration of the objectives set forth in this statement and of the best means of accomplishing those objectives.

Each statement is preceded by extensive discussions, meetings, and exchange of memoranda. The research is undertaken by a subcommittee, assisted by advisors chosen for their competence in the field under study. The members and advisors of the subcommittee that prepared this statement are listed on pp. xiii–xiv.

The full Research and Policy Committee participates in the drafting of recommendations. Likewise, the trustees on the drafting subcommittee vote to approve or disapprove a policy statement, and they share with the Research and Policy Committee the privilege of submitting individual comments for publication, as noted on page 175 of this statement.

Except for the members of the Research and Policy Committee and the responsible subcommittee, the recommendations presented herein are not necessarily endorsed by other trustees or by the advisors, contributors, staff members, or others associated with CED.

RESEARCH AND POLICY COMMITTEE (November 1986)**

*Voted to approve the policy statement but submitted memoranda of comment, reservation, or dissent. (See pp. 175-176.)

**This policy statement was approved by the CED Research and Policy Committee in November 1986

SUBCOMMITTEE ON FINANCE AND THIRD WORLD ECONOMIC GROWTH

Chairman
JAMES W. McKEE, JR.
Chairman of the Executive Committee
CPC International Inc.

ROY L. ASH
Los Angeles, California

RALPH E. BAILEY
Chairman
American Bailey Corporation

ROBERT H. B. BALDWIN
Chairman, Advisory Board
Morgan Stanley Group Inc.

HARRY HOOD BASSETT
Chairman, Executive Committee
Southeast Bank NA

JACK F. BENNETT
Senior Vice President
Exxon Corporation

JAMES F. BERÉ
Chairman and Chief Executive Officer
Borg-Warner Corporation

ROBERT J. CARLSON
Chairman, President and Chief Executive Officer
BMC Industries Inc.

RAFAEL CARRION, JR.
Chairman of the Board
Banco Popular de Puerto Rico

JOHN B. CAVE
Summit, New Jersey

ROBERT CIZIK
Chairman and President
Cooper Industries, Inc.

EMILIO G. COLLADO
Locust Valley, New York

W. D. EBERLE
President
Manchester Associates, Ltd.

JAMES B. FARLEY
Senior Chairman
Booz • Allen & Hamilton Inc.

JOSEPH B. FLAVIN
Chairman and Chief Executive Officer
The Singer Company

HARRY L. FREEMAN
Executive Vice President, Corporate Affairs and Communications
American Express Company

DAVID L. GROVE
President
David L. Grove, Ltd.

RICHARD W. HANSELMAN
Former Chairman
Genesco Inc.

CHARLES M. HARPER
Chairman of the Board and Chief Executive Officer
ConAgra, Inc.

HAROLD W. HAYNES
Executive Vice President and Chief Financial Officer
The Boeing Company

RALPH L. HENNEBACH
Retired Chairman
ASARCO Incorporated

RODERICK M. HILLS
Managing Director/Chairman
The Manchester Group, Ltd.

ROY M. HUFFINGTON
Chairman of the Board
Roy M. Huffington, Inc.

ALONZO L. McDONALD
Chairman and Chief Executive Officer
Avenir Group, Inc.

J. W. McSWINEY
Retired Chairman
The Mead Corporation

ROBERT E. MERCER
Chairman of the Board
The Goodyear Tire & Rubber Company

LEE L. MORGAN
Chairman of the Board, Retired
Caterpillar Inc.

ROBERT R. NATHAN
Chairman
Robert R. Nathan Associates, Inc.

LEIF H. OLSEN
President
Leif H. Olsen Associates, Inc.

DANIEL PARKER
Chairman of the Board
Omniflight, Inc.

JOHN H. PERKINS
Former President
Continental Illinois National Bank and Trust Company of Chicago

HOWARD C. PETERSEN
Radnor, Pennsylvania

PETER G. PETERSON
Chairman
The Blackstone Group

DONALD C. PLATTEN
Chairman, Executive Committee
Chemical Bank

EDMUND T. PRATT, JR.
Chairman of the Board and Chief Executive Officer
Pfizer Inc.

JOHN SAGAN
President
John Sagan Associates

ANTHONY P. TERRACCIANO
President and Chief Operating Officer
Mellon Bank Corporation

HAROLD M. WILLIAMS
President
The J. Paul Getty Trust

*Nontrustee Member**
JOHN R. PETTY
Chairman
Marine Midland Bank

*Nontrustee members take part in all discussions of the statement but do not vote on it.

ADVISORS

ANGELO ABDELA
Treasurer
CPC International Inc.

LAWRENCE J. BRAINARD
Senior Vice President,
International Economics
Bankers Trust Company

‡RICHARD N. COOPER
Maurits C. Boas Professor of
International Economics
Harvard University

FRANK W. SCHIFF
Consultant
Washington, D.C.

JOHN W. SEWELL
President
Overseas Development Council

JOHN J. SIMONE
Executive Vice President,
International Corporate and
Government Division
Manufacturers Hanover Corporation

PROJECT DIRECTOR

ISAIAH FRANK
William L. Clayton Professor
of International Economics
The Johns Hopkins University

RESEARCH ASSISTANT

PATRICIA POLLARD
University of Colorado

‡member Research Advisory Board

Purpose of This Statement

In recent years a spotlight has been turned on the Third World debt crisis and on related problems faced by developing nations. Much effort has been focused on helping debt-ridden developing countries solve their most urgent problems, such as servicing their huge external debts and making bearable the current hardships faced by much of their populations.

However, the CED trustees who undertook this study three years ago were not only concerned with overcoming the immediate challenges faced by these countries, they were also convinced of the need to look beyond the present situation to develop a financial strategy conducive to more stable, long-term growth in developing nations. The trustees realized that over the long term, Third World growth is critical not only to these countries but to the United States and the rest of the trading world as well.

One aim of this statement is to help decision makers in industrial countries understand the link between strong Third World growth and economic and political stability in their own countries. For example, in the United States, developing nations have become major trading partners and important areas for U.S. private investment and lending. At the same time, the United States and other industrial countries need to be mindful that their own economic policies have an impact on the prospects for growth in the developing world.

Recognizing these links, this report recommends a combination of more outward-looking, market-oriented Third World policies; industrial country efforts to stimulate growth and encourage a more open world economy; modifications in the programs and policies of private-sector lenders and investors in industrial countries; and improvements in official financing, both bilateral and multilateral, to help Third World nations use their resources more efficiently. The study presents both broad guiding principles and many specific recommendations for changes in financing programs, instruments, and governing rules. We believe this combination not only addresses the more enduring financial problems facing developing nations, but also provides useful guidance for the design of shorter-term measures to deal with the current debt crisis in these countries.

Acknowledgments

I would like to thank the business and education leaders who served on the CED Subcommittee on Finance and Third World Economic Growth for their diligent work and practical contributions. In particular I would like to thank Subcommittee Chairman James W. McKee, chairman of the executive committee of CPC International Inc., whose leadership, insight, and interest in these issues guided the subcommittee through to publication of the policy statement.

I would also like to acknowledge the outstanding work of Professor Isaiah Frank of the School of Advanced International Studies at Johns Hopkins University, who served as project director. His knowledge in this field and expertise in drafting the statement clarified many complex issues. Thanks also go to Research Assistant Patricia Pollard of Johns Hopkins University, who was of valuable assistance to Dr. Frank in compiling the necessary research.

William F. May, Chairman
Research and Policy Committee

Finance and Third World Economic Growth

1

Summary and Major Recommendations

The emergence of many of the poorer nations as highly dynamic elements of the global economy is a development that was hardly conceivable fifty years ago. Writers about the so-called backward areas typically saw most of them as irretrievably mired in poverty and stagnation because of conditions such as tropical climates that sapped human energy and local customs and values considered incompatible with the efficient use of resources.

The remarkable growth of many developing nations in recent decades is testimony to the enormous potential of the human and physical resources of the Third World. The most striking successes, including those of Korea, Malaysia, Thailand, Taiwan, Mexico, and Brazil, give hope to other countries, mainly in Africa, that are still struggling to establish the basic preconditions for self-sustained growth.

Unfortunately, many developing countries have experienced a serious setback in their progress during the 1980s. The worldwide recession, declining commodity prices, and the continuing struggle to cope with a heavy burden of international debt have all taken their toll in economic and social terms. At the same time, the flow of external capital to the developing countries has fallen off sharply.

The focus of this policy statement is on how to contribute to healthy long-run economic growth in developing countries, particularly through policies that will help to meet their needs for external capital in the years to come.

We believe that the time is especially right for major policy reassessments on the part of both developing and developed countries, commercial lenders and investors, and international lending and aid institutions. The changes we recommend focus on the long-term, but they also provide a guide for action in the short run that will help in resolving the current LDC debt crisis. Out of this reassessment can come new views, new policies, and new actions that encourage freer and more productive international flows of trade and capital that will benefit the North and the South alike.

In this policy statement special attention is given to the role that the U.S. private sector can play through the provision of both loan and equity capital. However, it must be emphasized that the effective use of foreign and domestic capital depends *primarily* on market-oriented and outward-looking economic policies in the developing nations and also on a world economic environment conducive to healthy and sustained growth.

For developing countries to position themselves for healthy, well-balanced economic growth, we believe their policies should be directed to achieve:

- Lower fiscal deficits
- A reduced role for state enterprises
- Realistic exchange rates
- Reduction of price distortions through greater reliance on market incentives
- Outward-oriented international trade regimes

The developed countries need to adopt policies to achieve:

- More rapid growth without inflation
- Lower real interest rates
- More open markets
- An increase in public flows of capital to Third World nations
- Resumption of adequate private flows of finance to the Third World

We also endorse a strengthened role for the multilateral financial institutions in:

- directly providing resources to the developing countries
- catalyzing augmented flows of private funds
- encouraging and supporting policy reforms in borrowing countries

In the long run, changes in policies along the foregoing lines will serve not only the interests of the people of the developing countries but those of the United States and the rest of the industrial world as well.

The Third World and the United States

In addition to its humanitarian concern for alleviating world poverty and suffering, the United States has a major ***political-strategic interest*** in promoting the economic and social development of the countries of the Third World. A reasonable pace of economic growth is necessary for the survival of developing country governments dependent on democratic support. Only the most authoritarian states can contain the frustrations bred by poverty and prolonged economic stagnation. With repression and stagnation there is a growing risk of political upheavals leading to radical regimes antagonistic to the values we regard as important. Economic and social development may not ensure stability and democracy in the Third World, but they are necessary conditions for sustained peaceful evolution of societies in which participation in the political process is broadly distributed.

The United States has an important role to play in strengthening international order. An expanding world economy in which the developing countries are active participants provides an improved international climate for the peaceful conduct of world affairs and for the resolution of issues in which this country has a major interest. Third World cooperation is important in dealing with problems such as migration and refugees, narcotics, international terrorism, population growth, nuclear proliferation, and environmental degradation. To the extent that economic and social progress causes nations to be more accommodating in their dealings with one another and more interested in cooperating for common purposes, the United States, as an active participant in the system, shares in the mutual benefits.

Until the 1950s, the U.S. *economic stake* in the newly emerging countries appeared quite limited. Third World countries were regarded as sources of raw materials and other primary products, as occasionally profitable areas for direct investment, and as secondary markets for the export of manufactured goods.

By the early 1980s, however, that relationship had been transformed. Although the developing countries remained vital sources of primary materials (especially oil) and important areas of direct investment, they also accounted for nearly 40 percent of total U.S. exports.[1] This exceeded combined U.S. exports to the European Community and Japan. Moreover, the developing countries accounted for most of the growth in U.S. exports between 1975 and 1980, far outpacing the industrial countries as expanding markets for U.S. products.

U.S. trade with the developing countries consists mainly of the export of machinery, chemicals, and agricultural products in exchange for primary products and low-cost consumer goods. Although expanding imports of inexpensive manufactured products such as shoes, clothing, and consumer electronics may cause structural adjustment problems in the domestic economy, they bring substantial benefits to the American consumer and help to reduce inflationary pressures in the United States.

In addition to their role as trading partners, the developing countries have become important for private investment and lending. Approximately one-fourth of the stock of U.S. foreign direct investment is in the developing countries, and more than one-third of all commercial bank lending from the member countries of the Organization for Economic Cooperation and Development (OECD) to foreign borrowers flowed to the developing countries between 1978 and 1982.[2]

The importance of a healthy industrial world economy to the growth of the developing countries is generally understood, but the reciprocal relationship is not so widely appreciated. The $17-billion drop in the annual volume of American exports to the developing countries from 1981 to 1983 resulted in the loss of thousands of jobs in the United States and exacerbated already severe domestic unemployment. During the same period, U.S. annual income from direct investment in these countries fell by more than $7 billion.[3] A substantial proportion of the increase in the U.S. trade deficit between 1980 and 1984 was due to the deterioration in the U.S.-Third World trade balance.[4]

The Third World Debt Crisis and Beyond

The outlook for growth in the Third World has been clouded by developments associated with the continuing serious international debt crisis (see "The Third World Debt Crisis"). Between the mid-1970s and early 1980s, private flows accounted for well over half of external financing for the developing countries.[5] Most of these private funds consisted of the surpluses of oil-exporting countries recycled through the commercial banks. As a result of the difficulties faced by the major borrowing countries in servicing their debts, net lending by private creditors has steeply declined, and its future course is uncertain. Moreover, in order to adjust to the current financial stringency, developing countries have had to adopt severe austerity measures that have kept their economic expansion far below potential, thereby aggravating internal social and political strains.

Although the difficulties facing the Third World countries have been severely exacerbated by the international debt crisis, most of their problems are of a more enduring nature. This policy statement therefore looks beyond the debt crisis and addresses the broader question of how to contribute to healthy long-run economic growth in the developing coun-

The Third World Debt Crisis

The onset of the debt crisis in the developing world is associated with the Mexican financial collapse of August 1982. Throughout the remainder of that year and into 1983, country after country, including the three largest Third World debtors, suspended normal debt servicing.

The severity of the crisis reflects both the magnitude of developing country borrowings and the adverse economic conditions that continue to confront some of the emerging nations. Between 1970 and 1985, long-term debt in the developing world rose from $68 billion to $711 billion. Including short-term debt, total external liabilities in 1986 were estimated at approximately $1 trillion.

By relating the debt to changes in nominal GNP, account is taken of both inflation and the real growth of GNP in the developing countries. On that basis the debt burden grew more modestly, from 14.1 percent of GNP in 1970 to 33 percent in 1985.

More important than the increase in outstanding Third World debt was the more rapid rise in debt service due primarily to higher real interest rates. As a percentage of exports, debt-service payments grew twice as fast as the ratio of total debt to exports. By preempting a large portion of export earnings, the high debt-service payments have become a major obstacle to the resumption of satisfactory growth in many developing countries.

The debt-relief operations that evolved following the onset of the crisis have consisted mainly of reschedulings in conjunction with adjustment programs under the auspices of the International Monetary Fund (IMF). They have been marked by difficult efforts to achieve compression of both public and private expenditures. In a number of countries, this approach achieved the intended results, but only at great cost in terms of slower growth, reduced living standards, and high unemployment. Mexico has proven to be a particularly severe case, in part because of the decline in oil prices.

The severity and duration of the crisis calls for innovative approaches to debt relief. Whatever these new approaches, they should embody two key principles: (1) a recognition (as in the Baker plan) that balance-of-payments adjustments must be combined with policies that foster long-run economic growth, and (2) a realization that the diversity within the developing world rules out a single sweeping approach to debt relief and requires programs tailored to the conditions of each individual country.

tries, particularly through policies that will help to meet their needs for external capital.

The Third World is made up of an exceedingly heterogeneous group of countries. In terms of per capita income, they range from Ethiopia ($110) to Singapore ($7,260). They vary widely in their reliance on primary commodity exports, their dependence on foreign capital, the size of their external debt, the literacy of their population, and their capacity to absorb modern technology.

From the standpoint of their reliance on external capital, it is necessary at the outset to distinguish the middle-income countries[6] from those at the low end of the per capita income scale, such as the countries of sub-Saharan Africa, where the basic physical and social infrastructure is typically still rudimentary. In the low-income group, the scope for private foreign lending and investing is limited, and primary reliance for external capital will remain on official sources for some time.

Flows of official and private finance from the industrial countries are essential for Third World development, but they are not sufficient. The effective use of both foreign and domestic capital is critically dependent on fundamental policy changes in the developing nations and on a world environment conducive to healthy and sustained economic growth.

Key Elements for Sustained Progress

Domestic Capital and Internal Policies

Economic growth depends on increases in a country's resources and improvements in the efficiency of their use. Capital is a key resource because of its relationship to the others: It provides the means of exploiting natural resources and improving the productivity of labor while serving as the main vehicle for technological change.

Most of the capital invested in developing countries is financed by domestic saving, not by inflows of funds from abroad. The reliance on domestic saving has been especially striking for the middle-income developing countries. Although it has varied greatly for individual countries within this group, domestic saving has financed on average more than 90 percent of domestic investment. A similar dominance of domestic saving characterizes the two most populous low-income economies, China and India, where much of saving takes the form of public surpluses. It is mainly in the low-income countries other than China and India that domestic saving has fallen far short of investment requirements. Moreover, in all but the poorest countries, domestic saving ratios have been higher on average than those of the industrial countries.

Despite the high levels of internal savings in relation to gross domestic product (GDP) in much of the developing world, there is evidence of a decline in recent years. It is essential that this trend be reversed, especially because domestic saving must compensate for the declining availablity of external financing and the high volume of interest payments on external debt. Among the principal measures required are reduction in budgetary deficits through cuts in government expenditures and greater encouragement of private saving through tax reform, moderation of inflation, and relaxation of restrictions on nominal interest rates.

Government intervention in the market may often distort the economy. For example, the overvaluation of a country's currency and exchange controls to stem the consequent outflow of private capital often only mask the deeper need for structural economic reforms. We do not advocate exchange controls even as a temporary measure. Rather than adopting such artificial devices, governments can utilize market-oriented approaches to relieve development problems. For example, a dual exchange rate system (temporarily legitimizing the black market) uses price to dampen capital outflow. Also, devaluing the currency leads to expenditure switching from imported goods to domestically produced substitutes, allowing for an eventual expansion of local industries and the generation of foreign exchange through increased exports.

Although it is theoretically possible for state-owned enterprises to operate efficiently, they are in fact rarely subject to the kinds of economic incentives that encourage efficiency in the private sector. In addition, there is an urban bias in the national policies of many Third World countries. For example, food price controls discourage agricultural production and investment, resulting in an unnecessary dependence on food imports. We recommend a reduced role for state enterprise and the encouragement of a market-oriented environment to better serve the economic interests of developing countries.

The widespread protectionist measures of the developing countries inhibit not only imports but exports as well. Although temporary measures to protect infant industries are sometimes in order, they often remain in effect for too long and allow inefficient industries to develop. Indeed, a number of studies have conclusively established a strong relationship between low levels of government intervention, expanding exports, and good growth performance.[7]

External Finance and Policies

Although domestic policies are the key to achieving Third World economic growth, aid and investment from the public and private sectors of the industrialized nations and a favorable world economic environment will continue to be necessary for the healthy development of many Third World countries. We recommend three types of action by the industrial countries:

- Expansion of capital flows to Third World countries
- More rapid economic growth in the industrialized countries, and in the United States, a special focus on reducing the deficit
- Removal of protectionist trade barriers

The flow of capital to the developing countries during the late 1970s and early 1980s was more than those countries could productively absorb. In the 1980s, however, they have experienced a real decline in both public and private sources of finance. With the severe contraction of private flows (even in nominal terms) since 1981, we believe that the pendulum has swung too far in the other direction.

The virtual halt in the flow of private loan capital has been an especially strong blow to middle-income developing countries because they rely more heavily on private sources of external finance than the low-income countries do.

The low-income countries, which have relied extensively on official aid from multilateral and bilateral sources, also need an increase in foreign capital to finance the physical and social infrastructure for long-term economic development. Because it is highly unlikely that private foreign capital will play a major role in these countries for many years, they will need to continue to be served mainly by official aid agencies.

In order for the developing countries to generate foreign exchange to service their debts and facilitate long-term economic growth, the industrialized countries must adopt policies to promote an economic environment that is beneficial to both parties. Most important, the developed nations as a group need to lower their interest rates and increase their own rates of growth so that new markets for developing country products can be opened and old ones expanded.

More specifically, industralized countries that have a strong external payments position, and sufficient control of inflation such as Japan and West Germany, need to adopt more expansionary policies. It is also essential for the United States to reduce its budget deficits in order to permit lower interest rates and to improve the trade balance.

The GDP growth rate in the industrial countries is not the only external factor affecting the ability of the developing countries to expand their exports. Equally important is the extent to which markets in the industrial countries remain open to Third World exports.

A disturbing tendency in recent years is the increasing resort by the industrial countries to discriminatory quantitative restrictions, often in the form of so-called voluntary export restraints and orderly marketing agreements. Unlike tariffs that an exporting country can overcome by increasing its productivity and reducing its prices, quantitative restrictions, such as those on textiles and clothing, place a rigid and absolute limit on the exports of developing countries.

It is particularly unfortunate that developing countries are being confronted with new obstacles to trade when many have undertaken difficult programs to adjust their economies to the realities of the current international debt situation and the shrinkage in new capital inflows. An essential element in most of the adjustment programs is the adoption of realistic exchange rates in order to make their products more competitive on world markets. But exchange rate changes can work only if the resulting shifts in price relationships between domestic and foreign goods can affect the flows of trade. By preventing these results from being realized, import quotas in the industrial countries frustrate the purposes of the exchange rate adjustments being urged upon the developing countries by the IMF and the World Bank. Such restrictions should therefore be avoided in the future, and existing ones should be rolled back.

To counter protectionist tendencies, the global trade negotiations should address the major issues affecting North-South trade. High on the list should be a gradual phaseout of formal and informal quantitative restrictions and a strengthened international safeguard code to deal with the problem of market disruption.

Official Finance

Official finance responds to a complex of needs in the Third World that cannot be adequately funded through private international capital markets, such as projects to develop a country's physical and social infrastructure. Conveyed mostly in the form of grants or low-interest loans, official finance provides the basis for an economic policy dialogue with the governments of recipient countries that often leads to reforms more important for development than the value of the direct aid itself. Our recommendations for policy reform in this area are addressed to four subjects:

- The size and nature of official U.S. aid
- World Bank policies
- Financing techniques
- The focus of multilateral and bilateral assistance

The United States provides approximately $8 billion a year for development assistance. Yet, as a percentage of the gross national product (GNP), U.S. contributions have been only 0.24 percent, well below the average of 0.36 percent for all the industrialized countries. At a minimum, current levels of U.S. official development assistance should be maintained at the 1983–1984 level of 0.24 percent of GNP, which would mean a rise from $8.7 billion to $10 billion today. We recommend that a portion of the increase should be used to enlarge funding for the International Development Association (IDA) of the World Bank, which provides low-interest financing for the world's poorest countries.*

The U.S. government has traditionally maintained that the principle of basing aid on a percentage of GNP is unfair because it fails to take

*See memorandum by Harold A. Poling, p. 175.

into account other ways (e.g., defense expenditures) in which nations contribute to the advancement of the international political and economic order. We urge nations (such as Japan) that devote a much smaller share of their GNP to defense to increase their overseas development assistance. Furthermore, in order to better serve overall security interests, we recommend that the United States examine whether at least some portion of the rapidly increasing U.S. funds for military programs in developing countries be channeled toward economic assistance.

Although bilateral aid is an important tool for achieving U.S. short-term strategic interests, multilateral aid retains a number of unique long-term advantages. We therefore welcome the return of the present U.S. administration to a more balanced approach to the use of both multilateral and bilateral economic assistance and, in particular, its increasing confidence in the World Bank as an instrument for development assistance.

The World Bank should remain the primary vehicle for channeling official aid to the developing countries. Its lending for projects, with their readily visible effects, remain the type preferred by many members. However, program lending that is used for general balance-of-payments support to encourage structural economic adjustments is generally a more effective instrument for basic policy reform. We believe that the Bank should have the discretion to expand nonproject lending beyond the present 15 to 20 percent of its aggregate operations.

In many instances, official aid may be combined effectively with private foreign capital. Cofinancing with private lenders allows longer maturities and better terms than strictly private loans while providing a less risky investment for private lenders. We support initiatives to increase cofinancing. In this regard, we believe that the Articles of Agreement of the World Bank should be amended so that a Bank guarantee of a private loan would count less than 100 percent against its capital, thereby reducing its own lending capacity by less than the full amount of the guarantee.

Unlike the World Bank, its affiliate the International Finance Corporation (IFC) has been involved in cofinancing since its inception in 1956. The IFC's mission is to stimulate private investment in developing countries by promoting and participating in the financing of profitable projects for which adequate capital is not available from other sources on reasonable terms. All its loans and equity investments are cofinanced with private domestic or foreign partners. To support the expansion and diversification of IFC's activities, its board has recommended doubling its authorized capital from $650 million to $1.3 billion. We urge Congress to approve this increase.

Although cofinancing is an excellent means for increasing capital flows to the developing world, the use of mixed credits by bilateral aid donors should be phased out. Mixed credits combine concessional aid with guaranteed export credits to provide loans on considerably better terms than market rates. This practice increased markedly between 1981 and 1984. However, such financing creates an unfair advantage for the provider and distorts international trade. Often, this device spreads because other countries feel that they must employ the same technique in order to stay competitive. We advocate an international agreement to eliminate the use of mixed credits and believe the United States should pursue efforts toward this end. Until that time, the U.S. Agency for International Development (AID) and the Export-Import Bank should be allowed to retain the authority to match credit terms offered by competitors.

In addition to the need for specific reforms of certain practices, we also believe that more general issues concerning official aid flows should be addressed. For instance, the flow of aid from the United States includes small amounts for so many countries that it is often impossible to be sure that it is being used effectively. Aid-financed programs should influence the overall policy environment in a developing country because this is a prime determinant of the impact that such assistance will have on economic growth. A related need is for aid flows to be better coordinated to maximize their effect. Ultimately, this will have to occur within the developing country itself.

Foreign Private Investment

Foreign private investment is an important source of capital for developing countries, especially in light of recent stagnation of official development assistance and the virtual halt in voluntary bank lending. Direct investment—the flow of capital from a parent company to its foreign affiliate—is most common. Portfolio equity investment, which denotes a share in ownership without involving the foreign investor in the actual management of the company, is another small but potentially important type of private capital flow.

Capital flows from direct investment usually take the form of equity; therefore, they are not part of a country's external debt. Also, direct investment is inherently long term in nature and better adapted than short-term bank loans to financing projects in which the returns extend over long periods. With direct investment, the capital source bears the risk involved in a project; in the case of a loan, the recipient bears the burden. Finally, the debt crisis and the conditionality of debt-relief operations have seriously undermined the view that private lending implies a lesser degree of external control than direct investment.

There are three principal policy areas that affect the environment within which foreign private investment operates:

- Domestic policies of Third World countries
- Policies of the industrialized countries in general and the United States in particular
- Policies of the multilateral institutions

Noninflationary, market-oriented domestic policies contribute to a more stable environment attractive to foreign investors as well as to a more efficient basis for allocating resources. However, many developing countries neglect the importance of stability in attracting foreign investment. They rely instead on special programs of incentives and concessions, sometimes at a high cost to the local economy.

Other policies often discriminate against foreign investors. The discrimination can occur outright by excluding foreign investors from certain sectors of the economy or by restricting the terms on which they operate. The restrictions work against Third World interests by discouraging foreign investment, encouraging the development of local industries for which the developing country may be ill-suited, and giving domestic enterprise a monopolistic position, inhibiting efficiency. However, recognizing that some restrictions on entry are inevitable, we believe that national treatment should be given to foreign firms once they are established.

Developing countries are especially concerned with protection of their infant industries and seek to shelter them from international competition. The trouble with this protection is that it is often indiscriminate in the industries favored, excessive in the degree of shelter granted, too long-lasting, and most important, overly reliant on direct controls. Unlike tariffs, direct controls such as import quotas break the link between domestic and international prices and prevent the market from performing its function as allocator of resources.

The policies of the industrialized countries must likewise be geared to promote the most efficient allocation of scarce private investment. When corporations shift investment to Third World countries because of a change in international comparative advantage, the United States should respond by helping displaced U.S. workers adjust. Specific recommendations on this problem are addressed in the CED report *Work and Change: Labor Market Adjustment Policies in a Competitive World*, released in December 1986. However, when U.S. companies relocate abroad because of an overvalued dollar or subsidies by foreign governments, the relocation becomes a distortion in the allocation of resources. In these cases, the U.S. government should act to eliminate the cause of the problem rather than treat the symptoms by restricting outflows of investment to developing countries.

The creation of the Overseas Private Investment Corporation (OPIC) in 1970 was an important step toward facilitating U.S. foreign private investment. OPIC offers insurance against the political risks of investing abroad and also provides small amounts of direct financing and credit guarantees. We recommend that OPIC's request for additional loan and guarantee authority be granted by removing the limit on the amount of its earned income that may be allocated to loans and guarantees after the provision for reserves.

The bilateral investment treaty program is a major U.S. instrument to improve the investment climate in recipient countries by providing a stable and predictable legal framework for potential foreign business. We support the program but believe it should be carried out in a more flexible manner. In recognition of the diverse circumstances of individual developing countries, the United States should be prepared to negotiate more limited commitments than those included in a complete bilateral investment treaty.

Patent and trademark abuse is a serious obstacle to increased foreign private investment. By reducing the ability of the industrial countries to recover costs, pirating undermines the incentive to invest in research and development. It also fosters continued technological dependence by developing nations. The U.S. government should urge countries to enact effective legislation for the protection of patents and trademarks and adhere to the Paris Industrial Property Convention.

The policies of investor and recipient countries are critical for the smooth flow of private capital, but the multilateral organizations can also play a useful role. One way is to help reduce the market distortions created by shortsighted national policies. For example, many host countries impose performance requirements on foreign enterprises that force an artificial increase in the volume of exports when minimum export targets are imposed or an artifical reduction in imports when local-content requirements are mandated. When the World Bank and the IMF give economic advice to developing countries, they should strongly discourage trade-related investment performance requirements. Moreover, efforts should be made in the new General Agreement on Tariffs and Trade (GATT) trade negotiations to develop new provisions to constrain the use of these devices by both developed and developing countries.

As a positive step toward encouraging private foreign investment, the World Bank's new Multilateral Investment Guarantee Agency (MIGA) will not only supplement the political risk insurance activities of national agencies but will also encourage host countries to adopt policies conducive to direct investment. We support MIGA in principle and believe its main contribution may lie not in its additional insurance facilities but in the confidence-building framework it could provide for host and home countries and private investors.

Additional steps to limit noncommercial risks are also desirable. In cases of the nationalization of business, the internationally accepted standard of prompt, adequate, and effective compensation should be applied. Furthermore, the laws of host countries and treaties between host and home countries should include these principles. To deal with disputes involving compensation for the expropriation of foreign property, investment agreements should contain a provision for recourse to international arbitration or other dispute-settlement mechanisms.

Sluggish growth and political instability in many Third World countries are major obstacles to a larger flow of portfolio equity capital, just as they are to direct investment. Even with improved general conditions, however, the potential for portfolio investment can be realized only if restrictions are removed and institutional improvements are made in domestic capital markets. Similarly, industrial countries should remove limits on the proportion of foreign equities allowed in insurance companies' portfolios, and public pension funds should be permitted to invest in foreign equities.

Commercial Bank Lending

The debt crisis that began in 1982 has severely hampered commercial bank lending as a source of finance for the Third World. Although it is generally conceded that private lending to developing countries in the late 1970s and early 1980s was excessive, we nevertheless believe there are reasons it should be expanded beyond today's depressed levels. The prospects will depend upon four factors:

- Improved domestic policies in debtor countries
- A healthier world economic environment
- Reforms in commercial lending practices
- Participation of the multilateral organizations

Clearly, government policy is important in determining the efficiency with which loans are utilized and the general creditworthiness of a country. Experience has shown that realistic exchange rates and the avoidance of excessive protection and subsidies are the best ways to discourage the financing of low-yielding projects. More prudent policies are needed concerning the level of borrowing (such as formal limits for public borrowing and greater regulation of private borrowing), particularly in countries where price, interest, or exchange rate distortions may encourage overborrowing. Developing countries should also maintain adequate levels of international reserves to allow for fluctuations in the world economy that may prove harmful to their ability to repay loans.

World economic conditions play an ever-increasing role in determining the prospects of individual developing countries. The slow recovery in Europe, where unemployment in some countries remains at over 10 percent, is associated with a number of practices that stifle investment and retard growth. Labor market reforms to ease the rigidities that have arisen in those countries are especially important.

In order to increase the flow of external capital to developing countries, we recommend the creation of a private insurance market to help cover the transfer risk on qualified loans. By spreading the risk, the vulnerability of the lending institutions would be reduced. In recent years, the huge drop in oil prices has severely hurt those debtor countries, such as Mexico, that have relied heavily on oil exports for foreign exchange. Because of Mexico's exceptional importance to the United States politically, economically, and socially, we recommend special measures of assistance to aid it in overcoming its present difficulties.

The debt crisis has exposed many weaknesses in commercial bank lending practices. New measures need to be formulated not only to overcome the present crisis but also to encourage more prudent bank practices in the future. The emergence of a secondary market for outstanding external debt is also conducive to augmenting the flow of new loans by increasing their liquidity and subjecting them to market discipline. Transferable loan instruments provide the means for transferring loan commitments by entitling the holder to receive interest and other benefits associated with the loan. Although they have been used only for industrial country loans, they could be used for Third World debt also.

The growth of the secondary market for discounted loans to developing countries should not be translated into pressure on the bank regulators to require that other loans to those countries on a bank's books be written down to market value.

We also believe that there should be more liberal tax treatment for loan reserves. At the same time that loan-loss reserve requirements have increased, tax treatment for these reserves has become less favorable. With the enactment of the new tax code, this treatment will worsen further.

To improve the ability of debtor countries to meet their loan obligations, commercial banks and multilateral organizations should better match the timing of repayment obligations with the changes in economic conditions that affect a country's ability to earn foreign exchange. Similarly, we recommend extending the coverage of the IMF's Compensatory Financing Facility (CFF), which is designed to provide loans for nations that experience temporary difficulties in generating foreign exchange because of fluctuations in the world economic environment.

The 1985 Baker plan is a laudable American initiative which recognizes that more than austerity measures are needed to solve the current crisis. A central element of the plan is the need for closer cooperation between the IMF and the World Bank in order to certify that individual debtor countries have met the standards that will qualify them as creditworthy. We strongly support the country-by-country approach to the debt problem because it takes into account the diversity of circumstances of individual debtor nations.

Furthermore, the World Bank and the IMF should encourage multiyear rescheduling of loans as opposed to reschedulings on a year-to-year basis. In this way, restructuring can be focused on the underlying economic problems of a country rather than the immediate financial problems associated with the debt.

Some observers have proposed establishing limits on bank lending either across the board or on an individual-country basis. Such limits would render some banks unable to participate in further involuntary loans for restructuring or encourage them to resist participation The alternative is the risk that limits would be set too high, encouraging future excess lending on the part of the banks. We therefore concur with the three U.S. regulatory agencies—the Federal Reserve, the Federal Deposit Insurance Corporation, and the Comptroller of the Currency—that country ceilings are inadvisable.

Concluding Comment

Our findings and recommendations are distilled from careful, wide-ranging study of the Third World financing problem. They look beyond short-term resolutions of current developing country difficulties to seek the underlying principles that should guide Third World finance. The detailed analyses and recommendations that support these conclusions may be found in the following pages.

The goal of this policy statement is to develop an effective, long-term approach to financing development in the Third World. Although we believe that the policies outlined in this statement will go far toward improving economic growth and living standards, we are also aware that the immediate and short-term difficulties many of these nations face in light of the debt crisis are very real.

Appropriate measures are needed to help deal with abrupt and sometimes wrenching changes in their economic and social situations. Many of the developing countries are experiencing great difficulties, but there is evidence that the debt crisis has opened doors for major reforms in policies that have long remained resistant to change.

2

Domestic Capital and Internal Policies in the Third World

Capital is only one of many factors affecting a country's prospects for growth. At the risk of gross oversimplification, it may be said that economic growth depends on the rate of increase in the resources at a country's disposal and improvements in the efficiency with which they are used. Both resources and efficiency have a domestic and a foreign dimension, but the domestic dimension is paramount.

In the classical definition, *resources* or *factors of production* include land (and natural resources more generally), labor, and capital. More recently, knowledge (or technology) has also been recognized as a vital productive factor. But capital is central because of its relationship to the other factors. It provides the means for exploiting natural resources and improving the productivity of labor and constitutes the major vehicle for technological change.

Domestic Capital

Early postwar writers tended to define the problem of development as one of capital shortage. Because poor countries could save little, their rate of investment was low. Low investment meant slow growth in output, barely sufficient to keep up with rapid increases in population. Sluggish economic growth, in turn, implied low savings rates. Thus, a vicious circle of poverty and economic stagnation characterized countries at an early stage of development.

In 1955, Nobel laureate W. Arthur Lewis wrote that "the central problem in the theory of economic growth is to understand the process by which a community is converted from being a 5 percent (of national income) to a 12 percent saver."[1] Because this conversion would inevitably be a slow process involving "changes in attitudes, in institutions and in techniques," the way to accelerate economic growth in the Third World was to supplement meager domestic savings by transferring resources from the rich, capital surplus countries to the poorer, capital-deficient countries. In short, foreign savings, mainly in the form of aid, were regarded as the key to breaking the cycle of poverty and low domestic savings and launching developing countries on the road to self-sustained growth.

In light of the capital-shortage conception of the development problem, it is instructive to examine current levels of domestic investment and saving in the Third World. A startling fact emerging from the data is that, in contrast with the situation in the early postwar period, domestic investment and savings ratios in all but the poorest developing countries are on average higher than those of the industrial countries.[2] The weighted average ratios for the middle-income developing countries in 1983 were 22 percent for investment and 21 percent for domestic savings, compared with 17 percent and 15 percent for the United States and 20 percent for both savings and investment in the OECD countries as a whole. Most surprising of all are the exceptionally high investment and savings ratios averaging 28 percent, for China and India, countries that together account for half the population of the Third World.

Even when allowance is made for the deficiencies of the data, the classical stereotype of Third World countries as low savers applies generally today only to the poorest countries of Africa and Asia (other than China and India). Broadly speaking, these are countries categorized by the World Bank as low-income economies and defined by per capita incomes of less than $400 in 1983. The most populous countries in this group are Bangladesh, Pakistan, and Vietnam in Asia and Ethiopia, Zaire, and Tanzania in Africa. Together, the low-income economies other than China and India have a population of 540 million, or about one-seventh of the developing world. As a group, their domestic savings rate, equal today to only 7 percent of GDP, conforms to the traditional pattern noted by Arthur Lewis.

During the 1960–1980 period, the developing countries have for the most part achieved remarkable success in increasing their savings. Only in the low-income African countries have savings rates actually fallen. In part, the decline was related to adverse movements in the terms of trade for exporters of tropical commodities: the amount of domestic production needed to pay for a given quantity of imports increased, leaving less for domestic savings. However, the decline was also related to high population growth rates and misguided government policies that led to falling per capita incomes.[3]

Although a high degree of diversity exists *within* the two Third World categories, low income and middle income, it is revealing to compare the groups in terms of average savings, investment, and economic growth experience. As the data in Table 1 indicate, domestic savings in proportion to GDP in the middle-income countries (20 percent) averaged almost three times that in the low-income countries other than China and India (7.5 percent). However, domestic investment in the middle-income group exceeded that of the poorer countries by a much smaller relative margin: 22 percent to 13 percent. The discrepancy is explained by the much larger role of foreign capital in financing investment in the poorest countries. Whereas external capital (largely in the form of official development assistance) accounted for more than 40 percent of total investment in the low-income countries, foreign capital (mostly from private sources) financed less than 10 percent of total investment in the middle-income countries.

Most of the more advanced developing countries depended heavily on external capital in the early stages of *their* development, and much of that capital was in the form of foreign aid on concessional terms. That assistance helped to lay the groundwork of infrastructure—transport, communications, health services, and education—that served as a basis for later development. As those countries continued to develop, they were able to rely increasingly on internally generated savings and to meet their proportionately reduced need for external resources through resorting to the private international capital market.

There is an association not only between the level of per capita income and savings and investment ratios but also between those economic indicators and rates of growth of total output. Between 1960 and 1982, the low-income countries experienced GDP growth rates of only 3.9 percent, compared with 5.7 percent for the middle-income countries. On a per capita basis, the discrepancy has been even wider: 1.1 percent for the low-income countries versus 3.6 percent for the middle-income countries. Thus, poverty, which is accompanied by relatively low savings and investment ratios, is, in turn, associated with slow economic growth.

It would be a mistake, however, to draw any simple causal relationship between the quantity of capital available to a country and its development performance. Averages often conceal as much as they reveal. Within each group, there is a wide range of relationships between investment ratios and GDP growth rates.

The quantity and quality of other available resources—labor, technology, and natural resources—affect the productivity of capital. Social, cultural, and religious factors also play an important role; they influence the framework of institutions and policies affecting the efficiency with which all resources, both domestic and foreign, are used.

A worrisome trend over the 1960–1980 period is the decline in the relationship between the growth of output and the rate of investment

Table 1

Growth, Investment, and Sources of Capital for Third World Countries

	Gross Domestic Savings (average of 1960 and 1982 as percent of GDP)	Gross Domestic Investment (average of 1960 and 1982 as percent of GDP)	Inflow of Foreign Capital (average of 1960 and 1982 as percent of GDP)	Foreign Capital (average of 1960 and 1982 as percent of Investment)	Average Annual GDP Growth 1960–82 (percent) Total	Average Annual GDP Growth 1960–82 (percent) Per Capita
Low-income economies other than China and India	7.5*	13.0	5.5	42.3	3.9	1.1
Middle-income economies	20.0	22.0	2.0	9.1	5.7	3.6

* This figure is an average of 10 percent for 1960 and only 5 percent for 1982.

Source: World Bank, World Development Report 1984, Annex Tables 1, 2, and 5.

in the developing countries. Despite rising investment rates to expand infrastructure, agriculture, and industry, the annual growth of GDP remained at about 5 percent for the developing countries as a whole.[4]

Declining returns on investment have profound implications for the economic prospects of the developing countries. One way to maintain growth rates in the face of such a trend would be to increase the rate of investment. However, if private flows of capital remain depressed and official aid flows do not expand, the increase in investment would have to come from a rise in internal savings.

Despite the high levels of internal savings in relation to GDP in much of the developing world, there is evidence of a decline in recent years.[5] It is essential that domestic savings be increased by reducing net dissaving in the public sector and by encouraging private savings through tax reform, moderation of inflation, and relaxation of restrictions on nominal interest rates.

Domestic Management

Although increases in domestic savings and external capital are necessary, equal emphasis should be given to the need for the developing countries to make better use of available resources. The decline in the aggregate productivity of investment in the developing countries has had many causes, including oil price shocks, deteriorating terms of trade, and the contraction of world markets resulting from the slowdown in growth in the industrial countries. (These and other external factors are examined in Chapter 3, "External Finance and Policies.") However, improvements in the overall efficiency of resource use depend in the first instance on more effective economic policies at home.

The state plays a pivotal role in the development process. It not only provides the social and physical infrastructure required for productive activities but also often engages in such activities directly through state-owned enterprises. The most important role of the government, however, is in establishing the policy environment for economic activity in the private sector.*

Macroeconomic Policies

A country's macroeconomic policies are a basic determinant of economic health. In many developing countries, loose fiscal policies accommodated by expansionary monetary policies have resulted in high inflation, over-

*See memorandum by Roy L. Ash, p. 175.

valued exchange rates, and huge current-account deficits financed by excessive foreign borrowing. By 1981, the combined current-account deficit of the non-oil-exporting developing countries had reached $109 billion (excluding official transfers).[6]

The principal domestic counterpart of the external payments gap and foreign borrowing was the rise in public-sector deficits. (Even where the public sector was not the borrower, the government was often the guarantor of loans to private borrowers because of lender insistence on some assurance that foreign exchange would be made available to service the debt.) By 1982, public-sector deficits had reached 10 percent of GNP in a number of developing countries and in certain cases even as much as 15 percent. Because of the undeveloped state of domestic capital markets, deficits on this scale could be financed only by the hidden tax of inflationary money creation or by foreign borrowing.

Primarily as a result of the fiscal deficits, high rates of inflation became common in most non-oil-exporting developing countries, averaging almost 30 percent annually between 1973 and 1981, compared with about 12 percent for the preceding decade.[7] Moreover, the depreciation of the nominal exchange rate tended to lag behind the differences between domestic and foreign inflation, resulting in an appreciation of real exchange rates and a deterioration in the current account of the balance-of-payments.

Capital Flight. In a number of developing countries, borrowing abroad had to finance not only current-account deficits but also private capital flight induced by unstable domestic economic and political conditions. That substantial capital flight has occurred is evidenced by the excess of cumulative international financing over the sum of recorded current-account deficits.[8]

In the late 1970s and early 1980s, capital flight was a major factor in the rapid accumulation of foreign debt in a number of countries, including Argentina, Mexico, the Philippines, and Venezuela.[9] The case of Argentina is especially notable. As its currency became increasingly overvalued, the inevitability of devaluation became widely recognized. To escape devaluation's effects, many Argentines bought U.S. currency, bank deposits, securities, and real estate. As a result, the $27-billion increase in Argentina's public debt between 1978 and 1982 was more than offset by the increase in privately held foreign assets.[10]

Many Third World countries have turned to comprehensive exchange controls as a means of stemming the flight of capital and preventing the exchange rate from being driven down. However, we do not advocate such controls even as a temporary measure. They distort the market and are often instituted as a substitute for necessary economic reforms. Moreover, controls are unlikely to be successful for long because the scope for circumventing them is wide.

A preferable alternative to exchange controls as a means of discouraging capital flight is to allow capital transactions to occur in a separate market through the use of a dual exchange rate system.* Outflows would be limited by a falling exchange rate for capital transactions rather than through the general licensing of outward transactions. By this legitimizing the "parallel" or "black" market, prices rather than quantitative government controls would dampen the capital outflow. As the international accounts of the country came into better balance, the free market rate would tend toward the level of the official rate and the system could be abandoned.[11]

The Adjustment Process. By 1982, the steadily increasing external payments deficits and the foreign borrowing to finance them could no longer be sustained. Net private lending fell off sharply, and most of it consisted of involuntary lending and the rescheduling of short-term debt under the aegis of the IMF.

The internal adjustments necessitated by the sharp decline in foreign lending took the form of reduced real expenditures through cuts in public budgets, increases in taxes, and the acceleration of inflation as a means of financing remaining fiscal deficits. These reductions in real expenditures brought an improvement in the balance-of-payments through a drastic compression of imports. At the same time, however, they induced a severe recession, with a wasteful contraction of real output and serious increases in unemployment.

This painful adjustment process can be eased by expenditure switching through a movement of the exchange rate to a more realistic level. Because a devaluation raises the relative prices of internationally tradable goods and services in domestic currency, it induces a reallocation of resources to the production of more tradable goods. One consequence is an increase in exports and a shift of domestic demand away from imports as their relative price rises and toward domestically produced import substitutes. Under this strategy, therefore, the burden of improving the balance-of-payments need not be borne so heavily by the reduction of imports but is shared by the expansion of exports. Thus, expenditure switching makes adjustment possible without the need for a severe contraction of real output.

However, whereas expenditure-reducing policies can decrease imports quickly, the effects of expenditure switching on the balance-of-payments can be perverse in the short run, and the benefits can take longer to materialize. Even in industrial countries, two or three years may be needed for the full effects of a devaluation to be reflected in trade flows.

---

*See memorandum by Leif H. Olsen, pp. 175–176.

The Structuralist Heritage

The central idea of the structuralist view is that market price signals induce only weak economic responses because of rigidities in the supply and demand for goods, services, and productive resources in the developing countries.

Economic growth was regarded as hampered by binding constraints. The shortage of domestic capital was due to the inherent weakness in the response of savings to changes in income and interest rates. But even if domestic savings could be increased, the resources released could not be transformed into foreign exchange because exports were regarded as exogenously determined by the level of foreign demand and were therefore unresponsive to changes in exchange rates and relative prices. At the same time, import requirements for intermediate and capital goods were deemed to be rigidly fixed by the level of domestic investment. Thus, developing countries were faced with two independent gaps or constraints on growth: a shortage of domestic savings relative to investment needs and a shortage of foreign exchange relative to import requirements. Only foreign savings (e.g., foreign aid) were considered capable of bridging both gaps because they simultaneously provided additional resources and foreign exchange.

Because of the prevailing belief in the inflexibility of the economies of the Third World countries, a deep distrust of the price mechanism as allocator of resources developed. Instead, its place was taken by comprehensive government planning and intervention, typically entailing large-scale direct public investment in state-owned enterprises, detailed regulation of investment in the private sector, and a high degree of protection of the domestic market, often through direct controls on imports.

In developing countries, it may take even longer for new investments in export and import-substitute industries to achieve their intended results. Nevertheless, the favorable results of this strategy are beginning to show not only in an improvement in the trade and current-account balances of a number of debtor countries but in the overall revival of their economies as a whole.

Microeconomic Policies

Appropriate macroeconomic policies are not sufficient, however. In many developing countries, major reforms are necessary in the state's role in the economy and the system of incentives resulting from widespread state intervention. Since the end of World War II, government policies in the developing countries have been heavily influenced by what has come to be called the *structuralist* view (see "The Structuralist Heritage"). This view favored extensive government intervention in the economy, state-owned enterprises, and a highly protected domestic market.

In most developing countries, the bulk of production in agriculture, commerce, and small-scale manufacturing is in private hands. However, large-scale manufacturing and mining (along with public utilities, transport, and communications) are often state-owned. Rarely can a public enterprise be made subject to the kind of incentives that will maximize efficiency. Noneconomic objectives, political pressures, bureaucratic procedures, and insulation from the discipline of competition and the risk of bankruptcy all tend to weaken the incentives for managers of state enterprises to minimize costs.[12] A reduced role for state enterprises would serve the economic interests of the developing countries.

A particularly critical account of how funds borrowed from abroad were used in the public sector was given in a World Bank report on sub-Saharan Africa:

> While part of these borrowings was used to maintain consumption when commodity prices fell (such as in Zambia), most of them went to finance large public investments, many of which contributed little to economic growth or to generating foreign exchange to service the debt. These projects covered a wide spectrum of sectors and countries. Examples include projects such as large conference centers, administrative buildings, university centers, hotels, and highways, as well as projects in the industrial sector, such as oil and sugar refineries, steel mills, and textile and cement factories. They occurred in low-income countries as well as in middle-income countries and most oil exporters. Clearly investment in social, economic, and political infrastructure is necessary, as is industrial investment and investment in service sectors (in hotels, for example). However, experience demonstrates that too much investment has gone into projects that have failed to generate significant increases in output. Genuine mistakes and misfortunes cannot explain the excessive number of "white elephants." Too many projects have been selected either on the basis of political prestige or on the basis of inadequate regard for their likely economic and financial rate of return.[13]

The low return on public investment in many African countries has been due to numerous causes, including inappropriate government policies. Part of the blame, however, must rest with the donor countries, especially their overzealous export credit agencies, whose main objective was to promote sales of home-country products rather than to assist in development.

In addition to direct public investment, governments often exert strong influence over resource allocation in the private sector through extensive intervention. The controls have included licensing investment, allocating credit, subsidizing interest, and allocating foreign exchange for the importation of capital equipment. Although some of these controls may have been justified in terms of the need to correct market failure, they have inevitably led to bureaucratic failure that biased investment away from agriculture and toward capital-intensive industries and processes in the presence of an abundance of cheap labor.

In the agricultural sector, intervention has commonly taken the form of price controls for food at low levels that benefit more politically active urban consumers. The consequence has been the discouragement of agricultural production and investment and a damaging dependence on food imports in the face of foreign exchange scarcity. This result has often been reinforced by land reforms concentrating on changes in tenure systems without adequate provision for the need of small farmers for technical assistance and credit for the purchase of fertilizer, pesticides, and other essential imputs.

Because more than 70 percent of the labor force of low-income developing countries is in agriculture,[14] perverse incentives in that sector are particularly damaging as they perpetuate poverty in the poorest countries. According to the chairman of the OECD Development Assistance Committee:

> Nowhere is there reasonable doubt today that the protection of consumer interests—mainly urban interests—through food price controls and indiscriminate subsidies has been excessive and self-defeating. In extreme cases crops have been extorted from farmers at below production costs. In many cases, producer prices imposed by state market monopolies have been a disincentive to smallholder production of surpluses for the domestic market. Their effect has been to suppress agricultural growth and rural non-farm development—the fundamental means of overcoming poverty in agrarian countries. This now deeply implanted error is easier to acknowledge than to correct.[15]

In many developing countries, political considerations make the simple lifting of existing price ceilings on agricultural products infeasible. One way to ease the transition from price limitations would be to allow market forces to determine producer prices but to provide direct government subsidies to urban consumers. This policy should be implemented only as an interim measure pending the full liberalization of the domestic agricultural market.

In developing countries that have adopted more market-oriented policies, agricultural output has often responded dramatically. India and Pakistan, for example, aided by the technological advances of the green revolution, have shifted from the position of net importers of food to that of virtual self-sufficiency.

Foreign Trade

Because development requires a rising volume of imports, countries must earn an increasing amount of foreign exchange to pay for their imports. Although external finance can help to relieve a foreign exchange constraint, the main reliance must be on domestic measures that remove the bias against exports inherent in highly protected foreign trade regimes.

High levels of protection at variable rates for different manufacturing industries have been common in the developing world. Often, the protection has been administered through complex quantitative controls and elaborate import licensing procedures. Where the controls were intended to protect infant industries, they tended to remain in effect long after any reasonable period of infancy. As a result, countries have been saddled with high-cost industrial structures incapable of competing in world markets.

Nor have the controls generally succeeded in improving the countries' foreign exchange situation. Because domestic products were far more expensive than comparable imports, the imports were sought through legal and extra legal means. Smuggling and black markets flourished. Moreover, the measures intended to discourage imports simultaneously discouraged exports. Restrictions on imports of intermediate goods raise the costs of finished products; protection also raises the cost of exporting by drawing resources toward industries producing for the home market and away from those producing for export. Perhaps most important, protection discourages exports by contributing to an overvalued exchange rate.

Yet many studies have established a strong relationship between export performance and economic growth for Third World countries at widely disparate stages of development. Table 2 shows the average annual growth of real export earnings and real GNP for selected countries for the periods 1960 to 1973 and 1973 to 1981. It demonstrates that those countries which have avoided excessively protective, inward-looking policies have achieved rapid export expansion that was, in turn, closely associated with relatively rapid growth of real income.

Increasing emphasis has been placed on encouraging trade between developing countries themselves (South-South trade). Although such trade has increased in recent years as a proportion of total developing country trade, further expansion appears limited by the lack of adequate infrastructure and the high trade barriers in the Third World. The inadequacy of infrastructure applies particularly to regional trade. There is a need to develop better intraregional transportation networks and marketing channels. Perhaps most important in limiting trade between the developing countries is the continued existence of high tariffs, extensive quantitative restrictions, and other barriers. Although import restrictions in the developed world have fallen substantially in the past thirty years, those in the developing world have not. Efforts to establish a system of trade preferences among Third World countries have met with much difficulty. Until barriers to trade are drastically reduced, South-South trade is unlikely to realize its substantial potential for expansion.

Table 2

Export Growth and Economic Performance for Selected Developing Economies, 1960-1973 and 1973-1981
(percent)

		Real Annual Rate of Growth				Real Annual Rate of Growth	
Economies	Period	Total Exports	GNP	Economies	Period	Total Exports	GNP
World	1960-1973	8.1	5.0	World	1973-1981	3.8	2.5
Economies with Balanced Trade Incentives							
Brazil	1968-1973	13.6	11.2	Chile	1975-1980	12.0	7.5
Hong Kong	1962-1973	13.6	10.1	Hong Kong	1973-1961	8.5	9.1
Ivory Coast	1960-1973	11.2	7.6	Ivory Coast	1973-1981	4.5	5.7
Korea	1960-1973	14.0	8.9	Korea	1973-1981	15.7	8.8
Malaysia	1965-1973	8.8	7.1	Malaysia	1973-1981	4.2	7.3
Singapore	1965-1973	12.6	12.7	Singapore	1973-1981	12.1	8.0
Average of Sample Group		12.3	9.6	Average of Sample Group		9.5	7.6

Economies with Inward Looking Policies

Argentina	1960-1973	4.0	4.1	Argentina	1974-1981	5.3	0.4
Chile	1960-1968	3.7	4.4	Ghana	1973-1981	0.0	-2.4
Ghana	1961-1973	1.5	2.7	India	1973-1978	7.7	5.1
India	1960-1973	3.0	3.5	Pakistan	1974-1981	6.4	5.4
Pakistan	1960-1973	2.9	6.2	Sudan	1974-1981	2.6	3.8
Turkey	1960-1973	7.3	5.9	Turkey	1973-1980	0.3	4.0
Average of Sample Group		3.9	4.5	Average of Sample Group		3.7	3.7

Source: Anne O. Krueger and Constantine Michalopoulos, "Developing Countries' Trade Policies and the International Economic System", (Paper prepared for conference of the Overseas Development Council, 28-29 September 1984), p. 5. Data from World Bank, World Tables, various issues; IMF, IFS Yearbook, 1984.

More generally, experience over the past couple of decades has demonstrated the adverse effects on growth of the complex of distortions associated with actively interventionist government policies. This experience has been bolstered by substantial empirical research on distortions in the prices of foreign exchange, capital, labor, and infrastructure services (particularly power). For example, the World Bank recently developed a composite index of price distortions of all types for thirty-one developing countries and has examined the relationship between the distortions and various components of growth during the 1970s. The results show a marked association between low distortion and good growth performance. Specifically, they reveal that those developing countries with low distortion indexes experienced more rapid growth in GDP, higher domestic savings rates, greater additions to output per unit of investment, and more rapid increases in exports.[16]

The New View

A new view has been gradually taking hold among students of the development process and practitioners in both national governments and international development institutions. These new ideas reflect a deep skepticism about extensive government intervention and a heightened regard for the effectiveness of free markets and economic incentives. In short, the notion that policy prescriptions based on standard economic theory are irrelevant to developing countries because of a complex of social, economic, and cultural rigidities is giving way to a conviction that many of the same prescriptions that work in industrial economies are highly relevant for much of the developing world as well.

The unfavorable international economic environment of the early 1980s underlined the importance of basic adjustments in the economic policies of developing countries. Because expanding balance-of-payments deficits could no longer be financed, a reasonable pace of economic development could be ensured only through improvements in the mobilization and use of domestic resources and in the ability of countries to transform such resources into foreign exchange. This has meant basic reform in domestic economic policies, programs, and institutions.

The thrust of much of the policy guidance of the World Bank and the IMF in conjunction with the Third World debt crisis reflects the view that traditional economic principles are applicable. With the tapering off in the flow of external resources to major debtor countries, increased emphasis is being placed on maximizing the yield from limited available resources. Although the focus of the IMF is mainly on short-term demand management, the Bank is encouraging longer-run changes in the structure of economies and in basic development strategies.

Structural adjustment requires different measures in different countries, but all these measures have a common denominator of less government intervention, greater reliance on markets, and the reduction of price distortions. Among the specific elements are the liberalization of foreign trade and exchange rate regimes in order to increase the competitiveness of production both for the domestic market and for export, the reduction or elimination of subsidies, incentives to increase productivity, and price policies that avoid favoring particular sectors. Discrimination against the farm sector in particular must give way to market pricing as an incentive to improved productivity.

Economic liberalization has its political counterpart. When the market, rather than bureaucrats, determines prices and the allocation of resources, tightly controlled political systems are bound to be undermined. This threat to existing authoritarian political structures is what often makes incumbent governments so resistant to economic reform.

Nevertheless, the responsibility for such reform rests in the first instance with the individual developing countries. Without the determination and cooperation of their government authorities, fundamental alterations of long-standing economic policies and practices cannot be achieved. But outside assistance, guidance, and occasional pressure can often help. The purpose is not to induce the authorities to take measures to which they are opposed, but rather to help them take difficult and politically unpopular steps that they know are necessary and in their country's long-run interest.

This role of external catalyst for domestic policy reform in developing countries is unlikely to be carried out effectively by major individual donor governments. Their motives are often suspect, their technical resources are often constrained by domestic considerations, and the relationship too frequently appears to be one of domination of the weak by the strong. Much to be preferred are the international institutions, especially the IMF and the World Bank, with their respective programs of stabilization and structural adjustment lending.

Policy reforms to improve efficiency are at least as important for successful development as increasing inflows of foreign capital. Moreover, considerations of efficiency do not, as sometimes implied, run counter to the achievement of a broad range of social objectives. On the contrary, the efficient use of scarce resources is an essential condition for reducing poverty, increasing employment, and widening opportunities for the people of the Third World.

3

External Finance and Policies

How a country manages its domestic affairs is the principal factor affecting its rate of domestic saving, its export performance, its attractiveness to foreign private capital, and its overall social returns from investment in the public and private sectors. Acknowledging the primacy of domestic policies in the Third World does not, however, relieve the industrial countries of their responsibilities for helping the poorer nations to realize more fully their economic potential. Sound domestic economic management is a necessary condition for satisfactory growth, but not a sufficient one in most developing countries. Adequate access to foreign capital on appropriate terms and a favorable world economic environment are also essential.

External Finance

The basic economic case for flows of capital from rich to poor countries is that capital is scarcer in poor countries relative to the supply of natural and human resources and therefore the marginal social returns to investment tend to be higher. Even in middle-income developing countries, where domestic savings have risen to high levels, inflows of foreign capital play an important role in achieving the expansion of output necessary to relieve the still widespread poverty of their populations.

In the low-income countries, especially those in sub-Saharan Africa, the need for external resources to supplement meager domestic savings is especially acute. Gross domestic savings in sub-Saharan Africa declined from an average of 15.5 percent of gross domestic product in the 1970–1975 period to only 7.5 percent in 1981–1982.[1] However, even if domestic savings rates recovered to their earlier level, the importance of capital inflows would remain greater than it is for most of the rest of the Third World. In order to satisfy the basic preconditions for directly productive investment, much of the capital will have to go into physical and social infrastructure. Because infrastructure projects typically have long gestation periods and generate nontradable outputs, private commercial financing is unrealistic. Most of this investment will therefore have to be financed through the public sector, including inflows of concessional finance from official sources.

Foreign Capital Requirements

The concept of *foreign capital requirements* for developing countries is elusive. In one sense, the need of poor countries for external resources is virtually unlimited. If we think of such resources as being used not only for investments yielding satisfactory returns but also for a spectrum of purposes that includes low-yielding projects and even consumption to raise living standards directly, the amounts required would be truly massive.

Given the constraints on the supply of world savings, any such sweeping concept of capital requirements has no practical operational significance. Foreign resources specifically for the purpose of increasing consumption directly in the Third World have been largely limited to relief in emergency situations such as earthquakes and famine. But external assistance for disaster relief should not be confused with foreign capital for development. The objective of development assistance is not to improve the lot of the people in poor countries by providing consumer goods directly but to contribute to better living conditions indirectly by increasing their own productivity and thus their real per capita output and incomes.

The need for development capital is limited by a country's absorptive capacity. The concept of *absorptive capacity* is not absolute but relative. It refers to the amount of capital that can be invested at yields exceeding some minimum socially acceptable rate of return. The lower the rate of return on capital deemed to be acceptable, the higher the absorptive capacity. Whatever the standard of acceptability, however, a country's absorptive capacity for capital is circumscribed by the inadequacy of other factors affecting the productivity of capital, including not only skills and management experience but also institutional limitations. The latter include such basic considerations as the extent to which law and order are maintained and the capacity of a government to plan and execute infrastructure projects and to provide the environment within which the private sector can function efficiently. (For a further discussion of the conceptual and estimation problems in determining foreign capital requirements, see "The Two Gaps" and "Estimation Problems").

Flows of Foreign Capital

Although estimation of future foreign capital requirements is a hazardous exercise, we can be reasonably certain of the extent and nature

The Two Gaps

Two approaches have been used to estimate the need of developing countries for external capital. Both begin by specifying target growth rates that theoretically reflect absorptive capacity and seem reasonable on the basis of recent trends. One method then focuses on the internal or savings gap (i.e., the gap between the volume of investment required to achieve the target growth rate and the supply of domestic savings). The other method focuses on the external or foreign exchange gap—(i.e., the gap between the imports needed to realize the growth target and the export earnings likely to be available to finance those imports). In terms of national income accounting, the excess of imports over exports is exactly equal to the excess of investment over savings; so in essence, the two gaps are simply different ways of measuring the deficiency of resources at a country's disposal. Although the savings and foreign exchange gaps become identical, they can and do diverge initially. The adjustments that convert resources released by an increase in domestic saving into an increase in exports or a decrease in imports take time to occur.

Moreover, the two gaps reflect somewhat distinct views of the ways in which capital inflows contribute to development. In the savings-investment approach, the shortage of investible resources is looked at as the limitation on development, therefore, the function of external capital is to supplement savings in the developing countries and thereby allow more investment than would otherwise be possible. The export-import approach emphasizes the shortage of foreign exchange as the effective bottleneck. The increased imports made possible by foreign capital may be regarded as performing a special function not merely by adding to the resources available to the developing countries but also by supplying specific goods and services that those countries are currently either unable to produce at all or could produce only at very high cost. If the lack of such imported goods prevents a country from utilizing its productive capacity fully, the productivity of the additional foreign exchange will be especially high.

of the reliance of developing countries on external capital in the past. The broad pattern has been one in which the middle-income countries have financed somewhat less than 10 percent of their investment from foreign sources, and the low-income countries other than China and India have relied on external capital to the extent of more than 40 percent. The pattern for China and India conforms more closely to that of middle-income countries. In the developing countries as a whole, the aggregate inflows of foreign capital over the past two decades grew at approximately the same rate as their GDP.[2]

However, the composition of the flows changed dramatically, as the data in Tables 3 and 4 demonstrate. Especially noteworthy is the reversal in the relative importance of official and private financial flows. Whereas official flows constituted more than 60 percent of the total in 1960–1962, private flows comprised almost 60 percent in 1979–1981. The emergence of private capital as the dominant source of foreign finance in the 1970s seemed a surprising development at the time. But it was anticipated forty years ago when the World Bank was established as a "temporary arrangement, to be superseded sooner or later by the re-

Estimation Problems

Whether foreign capital requirements are estimated in terms of the savings gap or the foreign exchange gap, they are inevitably based on arbitrary assumptions and subject to a wide margin of error. In the case of savings gap estimates, the bridge between the target growth rate and the required level of investment is provided by the incremental capital-output ratio (i.e., the investment required to raise output by $1). If the target growth rate of GNP is 4 percent a year and the capital-output ratio is 3, the required investment rate is 12 percent of GNP. However, if domestic savings are only 9 percent of GNP, foreign capital equal to 3 percent of GNP would be required in order to realize the growth rate.

Because external capital requirements are calculated as a residual, they are extremely sensitive to the size of the capital-output ratio. In the example, if the capital-output ratio is changed from 3 to 4, the total investment required rises to 16 percent of GNP, and the foreign capital needed more than doubles from 3 percent of GNP to 7 percent (16 percent minus 9 percent). Yet, historical evidence does not provide great confidence in the stability or predictability of the capital-output ratio. The reasons are the dependence of the ratio not only on changes in the productivity of capital as such but also on variations in the efficiency in the use of all resources (including labor and natural resources) as well as changes in the composition of investment in relation to the capital intensity of various sectors of the economy.

Large margins of uncertainty also attach to estimates of external capital needs based on foreign exchange gaps. In this approach, future export earnings of developing countries are usually derived from projections of GNP growth and import demand elasticities in the industrial countries for broad commodity groups. Import requirements of developing countries are estimated on the assumption that they are functionally related to variables such as national income, production in specific sectors, and volumes of investment. All such estimates are clouded by the difficulties of taking into account considerations such as import substitution possibilities in the developing countries, intensification of protectionism in the industrial countries, and changes in the terms of trade (i.e., in the relation between the prices of exports and imports).

Table 3

Composition of Net Financial Flows from DAC Countries to Developing Countries, 1960 to 1981

(millions of U.S. dollars)

	ANNUAL AVERAGES					
	1960-1962		1970-1972		1979-1981	
	Amount	%	Amount	%	Amount	%
Official flows	5,679	66.2	8,987	50.6	30,164	37.5
Private flows	2,903	33.8	7,810	44.0	48,082	59.8
Direct investment	1,697	19.7	3,883	21.9	12,872	16.0
Portfolio investment	642	7.5	1,781	10.0	24,728	30.8
Export credit	564	6.6	2,146	12.1	10,482	13.0

Source: J. Riedel, Myth and Reality of External Constraints on Development, Thames Essay Series, Trade Policy Research Centre, London, 1987.

Table 4

Average Compound Growth Rates of Net Financial Flows to Developing Countries, 1960 to 1981

(percent)

	1960–1962 to 1970–1972	1970–1972 to 1979–1981
Official flows	4.7	14.4
Private flows	10.4	22.2
Direct investment	8.6	14.2
Portfolio investment	10.7	40.4
Export credit	7.5	19.3
Total	**7.5**	**18.3**
Inflation rate*	2.3	12.0

* Rate of change of the unit value index of manufactures trade.

Source: J. Riedel, Myth and Reality of External Constraints on Development, Thames Essay Series, Trade Policy Research Centre, London, 1987.

sumption of lending from private sources." The World Bank is no temporary arrangement, but the resumption of large-scale private capital flows to the Third World was certainly realized, at least before the debt crisis struck in 1982.[3]

The composition of private capital flows to developing countries has also changed significantly. During the 1960s and early 1970s, direct investment was overwhelmingly the dominant form. Even as late as 1970–1972, it was more than twice as large as the flow of portfolio investment (mostly commercial bank lending). But by the late 1970s and early 1980s, the situation had reversed. Portfolio flows had increased in nominal terms at the astonishing compound rate of 40 percent annually during the 1970s, so that by the 1979–1981 period, this flow was twice as great as that of direct investment. Although the increase in direct investment lagged the expansion in other private flows during the 1970s, its growth nevertheless matched that of official flows (see Table 4).

Among recipient countries, the composition of financial flows varies greatly. Between 1979 and 1981, 90 percent of external capital received from Development Assistance Committee (DAC) countries by the major Third World exporters of manufactures was from private sources (see Table 5). At the other end of the income scale, the least developed countries have depended on official sources for more than 85 percent of their foreign capital. The remaining developing countries, those falling in between the most and least successful, received approximately equal proportions of external finance from official and private sources. However,

Table 5

Composition of Net Financial Flows from DAC Countries, by Selected Groups of Non-Oil-Exporting Developing Countries
(percent)

	Total Flows		Official Flows		Private Flows	
	1970	1979–1981	1970	1979–1981	1970	1979–1981
Non-oil-exporting countries	100.0%	100.0%	58.6%	42.8%	41.4%	57.2%
Major exporters of manufactures	100.0	100.0	31.3	9.8	68.7	90.2
Least developed	100.0	100.0	69.3	85.7	10.7	14.4
Remaining countries	100.0	100.0	65.2	52.4	33.6	47.6

Source: UNCTAD, *Handbook of International Trade and Development Statistics,* 1983.

all three groups increased the proportions of private foreign capital in their total receipts of external resources during the 1970s.

A somewhat different perspective on the composition of financial flows is given when Tables 5 and 6 are examined together. The data show that whereas private flows to the poorest countries account for an almost negligible proportion (2.8 percent) of total private flows to all developing countries (Table 6), such flows are not negligible (14.4 percent) when looked at as a percentage of all flows to the poorest countries (Table 5).

Recent Trends and Near-Term Outlook for Capital Flows

More recent and comprehensive data convey a vivid picture of the changes that have occurred in capital flows in reaction to the international debt crisis. Table 7 defines the total net flow of external finance as the current account deficit (exclusive of official transfer) of the non-oil-exporting developing countries (line 24). The rest of the table gives a breakdown of the four sources of finance for the deficit: official finance, direct investment, borrowing from the private sector, and use of reserves and miscellaneous short-term sources.

The volume of official financial flows has remained more or less on a plateau of approximately $42 billion since 1981, implying some contraction in real terms. However, direct investment, which had been expanding rapidly until 1981, decreased sharply in the ensuing recession even in nominal terms.

The largest and by far the most variable source of external finance since 1977 has been loans from commercial banks. Short-term trade finance from the banks to developing countries has existed for a long time; but in the years after the initial oil shock, this flow was first equaled and then exceeded by medium-term syndicated bank credits. As some countries began to experience difficulties in borrowing on medium-term maturities, they turned to non-trade-related short-term credits.

In the wake of the Mexican financial crisis in the summer of 1982, bank lending collapsed. It dropped from a peak of $82.4 billion in 1981 to $45.9 billion in 1982 and to only $16.5 billion in 1983. Most new credits have been in the form of *involuntary* lending (in Table 7, *concerted* loans). Under these arrangements, the banks collectively agree, along with the IMF and the debtor country, on the minimum amount of finance needed to support the agreed adjustment program, and pressure is then exerted on individual banks to participate in new lending in proportion to their outstanding exposure. In addition, there has been a massive rescheduling of short-term debt reflected in the $17.3-billion

Table 6

Distribution of Net Financial Flows from DAC Countries, to Selected Groups of Non-Oil-Exporting Developing Countries
(percent)

	Total Flows		Official Flows		Private Flows	
	1970	1979–1981	1970	1979–1981	1970	1979–1981
Non-oil-exporting countries	100.0%	100.0%	100.0%	100.0%	100.0%	100.0%
Major exporters of manufactures	24.2	31.1	12.9	7.1	40.1	49.0
Least developed	6.4	10.9	9.8	21.8	1.7	2.8
Remaining countries	69.3	58.0	77.1	71.0	56.2	48.2

Source: UNCTAD, Handbook of International Trade and Development Statistics, 1983.

negative entry for short-term bank loans in 1983 offset in part by an increase in medium-term debt.

In recent years, bonds issued in the capital markets of industrial countries have accounted for only a small fraction of private borrowing by developing countries. Bond flotations amounted to $3.2 billion at their peak in 1978 but declined drastically the following year. Despite this decline, bond issues have been holding steady at about $1.3 billion since 1981.

The "reserves and miscellaneous" category is typically negative, so that it is usually a competing use rather than a source of external finance. From this perspective, the most significant item is the buildup of foreign exchange reserves that had been severely run-down relative to need during the worldwide recession of 1980–1982. On the other hand, short-term drawings from the IMF became a major source of external finance during the recession and debt crisis. Given the revolving nature of the IMF's resources, however, this flow is also likely to become negative in the next few years as repayments exceed new lending. "Errors and omissions" is believed to consist mostly of capital flight.

The future needs of the developing countries for external finance are difficult to determine because they depend on both the internal adjustment process and the external environment. However, it appears that for the rest of the decade, their absorptive capacity for external financing will exceed the amounts envisaged by current supply projections.[4]

The extent of the excess absorptive capacity is an open question. Few would contend that the unprecedented level of external borrowing of the late 1970s and early 1980s is the right amount. Eduardo Wiesner, a former finance minister of Colombia and now director of the IMF's Western Hemisphere Department, argues that the level of borrowing for public and private purposes exceeded the capacity of the developing countries to absorb capital productively.[5] A similar view is expressed even by the chairman of the OECD Development Assistance Committee, whose task has traditionally been to encourage larger flows of external resources to Third World countries.

> It is not possible to judge the expansion of total resource flows in the late 1970s as unambiguously a "good thing." The 1981 financing level and the corresponding external balance of many of the major borrowing countries were clearly unsustainable. It would not be an appropriate or feasible undertaking to attempt to restore that peak flow of resources.[6]

Nevertheless, a substantial expansion of private flows above present depressed levels is needed to facilitate structural reform and to permit increased investment and more rapid growth in the middle-income

Table 7

Composition of the Net Flow of External Finance to Indebted Developing Countries, 1977 to 1984
(dollars in billions)

	1977	1978	1979	1980	1981	1982	1983	1984
1. 2 Official finance	$22.1	$24.5	$29.8	$36.6	$40.6	$43.4	$42.2	$42.6
2. Transfers	8.3	8.3	11.7	12.5	13.5	13.0	12.9	13.1
3. Bilateral loans	5.8	7.0	7.8	8.3	7.6	5.9	5.0	NA
4. Multilateral loans	5.7	6.5	7.1	9.3	9.6	11.9	10.2	NA
5. Export credits	2.3	2.8	3.9	5.4	5.7	-2.5	5.9	NA
6. Unallocated	0.0	-0.1	-0.7	1.1	4.2	15.1	8.2	NA
7. Direct investment	6.0	7.9	10.1	9.4	14.0	12.8	9.9	9.1
8. Private loans	28.2	43.9	47.3	61.1	73.1	49.3	17.5	13.4
9. Supplier's credits	2.3	3.3	4.0	1.8	0.6	1.0	1.4	NA
10. Bank loans	23.7	38.6	47.7	66.8	82.4	45.9	16.5	NA
11. Medium term	9.0	28.8	38.1	36.4	59.3	32.5	33.8	NA
12. Concerted	-	-	-	-	-	1.3	14.6	16.2
13. Short term	14.7	9.8	9.6	30.4	23.1	13.4	-17.3	-
14. Bonds	2.8	3.2	0.9	1.5	1.2	1.3	1.3	NA
15. Other	-0.6	-0.3	-0.2	-0.4	-0.1	-0.1	-0.1	NA

16. Reserves and miscellaneous	-19.4	-20.4	-30.5	-38.6	-26.1	-1.3	-11.8	-27.4
17. Change in reserves (Increase = -)	-10.7	-13.5	-21.5	-18.4	1.6	14.4	-9.5	-22.3
18. SDR allocations*	0.6	1.4	2.9	2.5	0.5	2.9	0.1	0.5
19. Reserve creation†	2.0	1.4	-1.3	1.9	0.9	1.1	-1.3	-0.2
20. Export credit extended by developing countries††	-6.2	-4.9	-7.8	-7.8	-17.4	-12.9	-8.2	-5.8
21. Borrowing from IMF	-0.2	-0.4	0.2	1.5	6.0	7.0	11.0	5.3
22. Change in arrears (Increase = +)	1.6	0.5	0.4	0.8	2.0	11.1	7.5	-1.3
23. Errors and omissions	-6.5	-4.9	-3.4	-19.1	-19.7	-24.9	-11.4	-3.6
24. Current account deficit on goods, services and private transfers	36.9	56.8	61.7	77.0	112.9	102.9	59.4	37.9

- = Negligible.

NA = Not Available.

* Special drawing rights (SDR) allocations, valuation adjustments, and gold monetization.

† Short-term borrowing by monetary authorities from other monetary authorities excluding the IMF.

†† Described as "asset transactions, net" by World Economic Outlook.

Source: Donald R. Lessard and John Williamson, Financial Intermediation Beyond the Debt Crisis (Washington, D.C.: Institute for International Economics, 1985).

countries. Larger official flows are also required, including a higher volume of concessional aid, to help resolve the serious development problems of the poorer countries.

External Policies

The growth prospects of developing countries depend on far more than the availability of external finance. Domestic policies are of critical importance because they affect both the supply of internal savings and the efficiency with which all resources, both internal and external, were used. Nevertheless, the external environment matters a great deal, especially the economic policies of the industrial countries.

A Look Back

It is clear that the policy responses of the industrial countries to the two oil price shocks of the 1970s contributed to the debt crisis in the developing countries and to the painful economic adjustments of the 1980s, which has come to be called the *lost decade.* The initial round of increases in oil prices in 1973–1974 meant a transfer of income to the members of the Organization of Petroleum Exporting Countries (OPEC) that induced a recession in the industrial world in 1974–1975. The response of the industrial countries was to adopt expansionary monetary policies that, when combined with the direct and indirect price effects of the OPEC action, gave a strong impetus to inflation. Average inflation rates increased from 4.7 percent in 1963–1972 to more than 10 percent in 1974–1975. Real interest rates turned sharply negative in 1974 and remained virtually at zero through the end of the decade. With financing costs so cheap, it is understandable that developing countries chose to borrow heavily in order to avoid the real adjustment to higher oil prices that would have undermined development programs.

The policy response of the industrial countries to the second oil shock in 1979–1980 was very different. Expansionary policies were avoided in favor of tightened monetary policy in order to counter inflation. This policy, combined with high inflationary expectations drove up real interest rates to almost 10 percent in 1981 and contributed to the worldwide recession of 1981–1983. There is little doubt that this sharp reversal of monetary policy in the United States exacerbated the severe debt problems of the developing countries both by reducing their export earnings and by increasing the cost of debt service.

A Look Ahead

The sensitivity of developing country economic prospects to the performance of the industrial countries is demonstrated by alternative growth scenarios constructed by the World Bank for the 1985–1995 period.[7] The "Low Case" indicates what might happen if the industrial countries' performance merely replicated that of the past ten years, especially in terms of slow growth and high interest rates. Unemployment would remain high, and protectionist sentiment would be strong. Exports from developing countries would expand only slowly, loans from private sources would be severely limited, and overall growth in Third World per capita income would be only 2.7 percent a year. For the low-income countries of Africa, the results would be especially serious, per capita GDP would decline at the annual rate of 0.5 percent.

The "High Case" is predicated on a path of sustained GDP expansion for the industrial countries at a rate of 4.3 percent. Unemployment would then fall steadily. This scenario also assumes that U.S. budget deficits would be gradually reduced, first as a proportion of GDP, then in absolute terms. With deficits under control, real interest rates would fall to 2.5 percent from the 1980–1985 level of 5.2 percent. The consequences for the developing countries are summarized as follows: "As unemployment eases, protectionist measures subside, so developing countries would find it easier to expand their exports and ease their debt service burden. Investment confidence would rapidly improve, which, along with larger aid programs, would lead to an expansion of the flows of capital to developing countries."[8]

Implications

What emerges from both the historical record and the projections is the crucial importance of faster, more stable growth and lower real interest rates in the industrial countries in resolving the debt problems and restoring more satisfactory growth in the developing countries. In terms of policy, this implies a need to reduce budgetary deficits in the United States in order to permit somewhat more expansionary monetary policy and lower interest rates. In other OECD countries with strong payments positions and sufficient control of inflation, macroeconomic expansion is in order, but with varying policy mixes. For example, Japan and Germany could adopt more expansionary policies to stimulate faster growth and a more sustainable world payments balance.[9]

U.S. macroeconomic policies affect developing countries not only through the cost of capital but also through the amount available to them. By attracting foreign capital, high U.S. interest rates have contributed to a strong dollar. The 40.3 percent real trade-weighted appreciation of the dollar between 1980 and early 1985[10] was a major cause of the U.S. current-account deficit, which reached $118 billion in 1985. That deficit, which was financed by capital imports, exceeded the maximum combined deficit of all the developing countries in 1981. Thus, a substantial share of the world's savings represented by the counterpart of the deficit, the current-account surpluses of other countries (mainly Japan and West Germany), is being absorbed in the form of massive imports of capital by the United States.

The foreign exchange value of the dollar reached its peak in February 1985.[11] Nevertheless, it is still above 1980 levels, when the U.S. current account was substantially in equilibrium. Although the decline in the dollar will result in an improvement in the U.S. trade account, the balance is likely to remain strongly in deficit for some time because of the present 50 percent excess of imports over exports. Furthermore, any improvement in the current account will be dampened by the rise in net investment income accruing to other countries.

It is sometimes argued that a rich country such as the United States should not be running a large external deficit because it drains much-needed capital from the rest of the world, especially the developing countries. However, the seriousness of the matter depends on the extent to which the rest of the world is close to full employment. If the world were in that situation, there would be little scope for enlarging the supply of savings through an expansion of income. So long as high levels of unemployment and excess capacity exist in the rest of the industrial world, there is room for economies to expand and savings to rise. The drain of world savings to the United States can therefore still be offset to some extent by rising income and savings abroad.[12]*

Protection

The capacity of Third World countries to import products needed for development depends on the availability of foreign exchange to pay for the imports. As a source of foreign exchange, their exports (other than oil) are almost ten times as large as the total flows of bilateral and multilateral financial assistance from the United States, Japan, and Western Europe. A 10 percent decline in exports, therefore, would virtually wipe out the foreign exchange equivalent of all current official aid flows from the industrial countries. We must not permit protection to expose the developing countries to that hazard.

The economic growth of the developing countries is strongly correlated with their export performance, and the importance of increasing exports from the developing countries is especially acute in light of their debt problems. With the volume of net lending sharply curtailed, there is no

---

*See memorandum by Leif H. Olsen, p. 176.

way that the major debtors can pay even the interest on their existing external debt except by running trade surpluses. Until recently, they have accomplished this mainly by cutting imports in the context of severe austerity programs. If the economic recovery of those countries is to be sustained, they will have to achieve a trade surplus by boosting their exports.

The ability of developing countries to expand their exports depends in the first instance on their own policies that affect their response to market opportunities abroad. But the rate of economic growth in the industrial countries and the extent to which their markets remain open to Third World exports are also critically important.

What is especially disturbing is the tendency in recent years for the industrial countries to resort to discriminatory nontariff restrictions of the quantitative variety, often in the form of so-called voluntary export restraints and orderly marketing agreements. Unlike tariffs that an exporting country can overcome by increasing its productivity and lowering its prices, quantitative restrictions place a rigid and absolute bar to exports. The tighter import quotas recently placed by the United States on textiles and apparel as well as on steel are an ominous sign.* Such restrictions are even more severe in Europe and Japan, where nontrade subsidies to domestic industry also adversely affect the export prospects of developing countries. The European Community's common agricultural policy has had particularly harmful effects in reducing the market in Europe for Third World agricultural exports and displacing developing country exports (e.g., sugar) to third countries.

It is particularly unfortunate that developing countries are being confronted with new obstacles to trade at a time when many have undertaken difficult programs to adjust their economies to the realities of the current international debt situation and the shrinkage in new capital inflows. An essential element in most of these adjustment programs is the adoption of a realistic exchange rate in order to make their products more competitive on world markets. But exchange rate changes can work only if the resulting shifts in price relationships between domestic and foreign goods can affect the flows of trade. By preventing these results from being realized, import quotas and other forms of quantitative restrictions frustrate the purposes of the exchange rate adjustments being urged upon the developing countries by the IMF and the World Bank. Such measures should therefore be avoided.

Trade restrictions by the industrial countries are not only harmful to the developing nations; they are also costly to the countries imposing

---

*See memorandum by W. Bruce Thomas, p. 176.

them. We therefore endorse the recent proposal of the GATT "Wise Men" that the costs and benefits to the national economy of existing and prospective trade policy actions should be analyzed through a "protection balance sheet."[13] If this idea were adopted, it would improve the quality of public discussion by showing the trade-offs in any protectionist action and would also help to strengthen the constituency in favor of open trade policies.

Trade and aid are complementary ways of providing developing countries with the means to import the products required for development. But there is an essential difference between the two: Aid entails a sacrifice by the donor; trade is mutually beneficial to both sides of the transaction. When a country liberalizes or removes a barrier to imports, it helps not only the foreign exporter but itself as well.

To counter protectionist tendencies, the global trade negotiations should comprehend the major issues affecting North-South trade. High on the list should be a gradual phaseout of formal and informal quantitative restrictions and a strengthened international safeguard code to deal with the problem of market disruption.

4

Official Finance

Official development finance plays a distinctive role in the structure of international capital flows. In addition to promoting growth in the Third World, it is motivated at least in part by a humanitarian desire to improve the well-being of the poor. When conveyed bilaterally, it often also reflects special political, economic, or cultural ties between the donor and particular recipient countries or groups of countries. However, official finance also responds to a complex of economic needs in the Third World that cannot be met adequately through the international private capital markets.

Economic Role of Official Finance

Although the returns on investment in the developing countries may be high, the time preference and traditional practices of capital markets limit the availability of long-term funding through private channels. Many of the investments needed to overcome the basic obstacles to economic growth are in physical infrastructure such as roads and power and in fields such as health, education, and agricultural research. Because the payoff from these investments may be spread very broadly through society and realized only over a long period (perhaps thirty to forty years), with only limited returns in the early years, they are generally considered unsuitable for private financing.

Most official finance is conveyed on concessional terms in the form of outright grants or low-interest loans. It therefore involves little or no debt-service obligation. Almost three-fifths of concessional finance goes to countries with per capita incomes below $700.[1] The concessionality reflects recognition of the limited capacity of the poorer countries to capture the benefits of investments in physical and social infrastructure and to convert those gains into foreign exchange to service debt.

Official finance can also be distinguished from private capital flows in providing the basis for an economic policy dialogue with the governments of recipient countries as well as technical advice designed to improve their overall development performance. By raising the productivity of existing resources, the policy adjustments and reforms adopted in conjunction with aid programs are often as important as, or even more important than, the increment in resources itself.

Composition and Trends in Official Finance

There are two broad groups of official sources of finance: official development assistance and other official flows. The distinction is that official development assistance must satisfy two conditions: (1) Its main objective must be the promotion of economic development; (2) The resources must be made available at terms reflecting at least an agreed minimum degree of concessionality.[2]

Official development assistance takes many forms, including grants in the form of cash, debt forgiveness, technical assistance, food, and loans at below-market rates. Official export credits, even if they meet the concessional criterion, are not included if their primary purpose is export promotion rather than development. On the other hand, loans by the World Bank from its regular resources meet the development criterion but are excluded because they lack the required degree of concessions.

A measure of the concessional nature of a loan is its grant element. This depends on the difference between the actual interest rate charged and the market rate as well as on the grace period and maturity of the loan. To qualify as official development assistance, a loan must have a grant element of at least 25 percent.[3] However, the real volume of aid is reduced to the extent that the donor ties the aid by requiring the recipient to import from the donor country and the donor's prices exceed world market prices. The softer the terms of aid and the less the aid is tied, the greater its value to the recipient.

The DAC established an 86 percent grant element as a target for each member's total annual official development aid program. In 1983 and 1984, the average grant element of DAC members' official development assistance exceeded 90 percent. However, Austria and Japan failed to reach the target rate in either year, and Germany slipped slightly below the target in 1984 (see Table 8).

Over the 1970–1985 period, official finance (both development assistance and other flows) accounted for between one-third and over two-thirds of all financial flows (official and private) from DAC countries to the nations of the Third World. Of \$32.8 billion of official DAC flows in 1985, \$29.4 billion (90 percent) was on sufficiently concessional terms to be classified as development assistance (see Table 9). In addition, the members of OPEC provided about \$3.5 billion of development assistance,

Table 8

Grant Element of Official Development Assistance Commitments[a]
(percent)

Country	1983	1984
Australia	100.0	100.0
Austria	61.0	82.1
Belgium	97.3	98.1
Canada	99.3	98.6
Denmark	96.4	98.0
Finland	99.7	95.6
France	89.3	88.4
Germany	88.8	84.6
Italy	90.7	91.2
Japan	79.8	73.7
Netherlands	95.1	93.4
New Zealand	100.0	100.0
Norway	98.1	99.4
Sweden	99.8	100.0
Switzerland	98.5	98.1
United Kingdom	98.3	99.4
United States	94.7	93.7
Total DAC countries	91.3	90.0

[a] The target is 86 percent.

Source: OECD, Twenty-Five Years of Development Cooperation: 1985 Report, p. 107.

Table 9

Net Flow of Financial Resources from DAC Countries to Developing Countries and Multilateral Agencies[a]
(dollars in millions)

	AMOUNT								PERCENT							
	1970	1975	1980	1981	1982	1983	1984	1985	1970	1975	1980	1981	1982	1983	1984	1985
Official development assistance	6,949	13,854	27,297	25,540	27,731	27,593	28,729	29,419	44	31	36	28	33	39	34	61
Other official flows	1,122	3,912	5,270	6,606	7,414	4,884	6,196	3,413	7	9	7	7	9	7	7	7
Private flows	7,018	25,706	40,403	57,210	46,557	35,355	47,271	12,797	44	57	54	63	55	51	56	26
Grants by private voluntary agencies	860	1,346	2,386	2,005	2,317	2,344	2,584	2,842	5	3	3	3	3	3	3	6
Total net flows	15,948	44,817	75,356	91,362	84,018	70,176	84,779	48,472	100	100	100	100	100	100	100	100

[a] Net disbursements at current prices and exchange rates.

Source: OECD, Twenty-Five Years of Development Cooperation: 1985 Report, p. 331 (for 1981 and 1982); Draft DAC Chairman's Report for 1986, Statistical Annex, Table 4, p. 15 (DAC(86)46, September 23, 1986), for 1975, 1980, 1983-85.

and the Soviet bloc provided about $3.2 billion, mostly to Vietnam and Cuba. Of total official development assistance receipts from all sources, about 78 percent is conveyed bilaterally; the rest flows through multilateral agencies such as the World Bank and the regional development banks (see Table 10).

As the data in Table 10 indicates, the aggregate real flow of official development assistance virtually stagnated between 1978 and 1985. Thus, there has been practically no offset in the trend of official flows to the sharp contraction in private financial flows since 1981.[4]

To the extent that flows of official finance are inadequate, the problems posed for the developing countries are exacerbated. Given the heavy reliance of the poorest countries on concessional finance, the impact on them will be particularly severe. More generally, however, it will mean more drastic economic retrenchment, with the loss of opportunities to use existing resources and capacity more fully and efficiently. Reducing the level of investment will adversely affect long-term economic development in the Third World. This would mean not only greater hardship for the inhabitants of the developing countries but also a loss of efficiency and a drag on growth for the world economy as a whole.

U.S. Economic Assistance

The U.S. economic assistance program has a wide range of goals that are not always mutually consistent: meeting emergency needs in the world's poorest countries; advancing U.S. strategic and political interests; promoting economic development in the Third World; and expanding U.S. exports. In recent years, the program has become increasingly oriented toward security goals, with assistance heavily concentrated in countries where U.S. political and strategic interests are regarded as threatened by the Soviet Union or its proxies.

U.S. economic assistance is, for budgetary purposes, part of a broader foreign aid program that encompasses military assistance as well. Although the economic component has stagnated in terms of volume, the military portion has increased substantially. The United States should examine whether its overall security interests would be better served by channeling a share of the military program funds to economic assistance.

An average of $8.6 billion was provided annually by the United States for economic assistance between 1981 and 1984. About 90 percent of that amount qualified in terms of concessionality to be included in official development assistance. Close to 75 percent of U.S. aid was conveyed bilaterally in 1984; the rest was channeled through the multilateral development institutions.[5]

Table 10

Total Net Resource Flows to Developing Countries by Major Types of Flows[a]
(dollars in billions)

TYPE OF FLOW	AMOUNT									PERCENT		
	1975	1976	1979	1980	1981	1982	1983	1984	1985	1975	1980	1985
I. OFFICIAL DEVELOPMENT FINANCE (ODF)	**37.3**	**36.4**	**37.5**	**42.1**	**44.2**	**43.7**	**41.4**	**47.3**	**47.6**	**44.8**	**35.3**	**60.0**
Official development assistance (ODA)	30.9	30.5	31.8	34.7	35.4	33.1	33.0	34.6	34.9	37.1	29.2	44.1
Bilateral	25.4	24.5	25.5	27.5	27.9	25.8	25.6	26.8	27.5	30.5	23.1	34.7
OECD countries	12.0	14.8	16.6	16.8	17.6	18.2	18.3	19.8	21.9	14.4	14.1	27.6
OPEC countries	8.3	7.4	6.5	8.0	7.2	4.4	3.8	3.7	2.3	10.0	6.7	2.9
CMEA countries	2.2	1.8	2.1	2.5	2.9	2.9	3.1	3.0	3.1	2.6	2.1	3.9
Other countries	0.6	0.6	0.3	0.3	0.3	0.3	0.3	0.3	0.3	0.7	0.2	0.4
Multilateral	5.5	6.0	6.2	7.2	7.5	7.3	7.4	7.8	(7.4)	6.7	6.0	(9.4)
Other ODF	6.4	5.9	5.7	7.4	8.8	10.5	8.4	12.7	12.7	7.7	6.2	16.0
of which: Multilateral	3.6	3.4	4.1	4.4	5.4	6.4	7.0	8.2	8.7	4.4	3.7	11.0
Bilateral	2.8	2.4	1.6	2.9	3.3	4.1	1.4	4.5	4.0	3.3	2.5	5.0

II. TOTAL EXPORTS CREDITS	**8.2**	**16.9**	**13.8**	**16.1**	**17.2**	**14.1**	**8.1**	**5.4**	**3.0**	**9.8**	**13.5**	**3.7**
OECD countries	8.2	16.7	13.5	15.4	16.2	13.4	7.6	5.0	2.6	9.8	12.9	3.2
of which: short term	-	2.9	2.0	2.2	2.5	2.9	-0.3	-0.8	-	-	1.9	-
Other countries	-	0.2	0.3	0.7	1.0	0.7	0.5	0.4	0.4	-	0.6	0.5
III. PRIVATE FLOWS	**37.8**	**67.9**	**56.1**	**60.9**	**70.9**	**57.0**	**45.9**	**30.2**	**28.7**	**45.4**	**51.1**	**36.2**
Direct investment (OECD)	16.6	13.2	13.5	10.3	16.4	12.5	9.1	10.4	7.9	20.0	8.7	10.0
International bank sector	17.5	44.3	35.9	45.1	49.6	40.0	33.4	17.4	12.9	21.0	37.9	16.2
of which: short-term	-	18.9	16.1	24.0	21.0	14.7	-12.7	-6.0	-5.9	0.0	20.1	-7.5
Total bond lending	0.6	4.6	2.0	1.5	1.2	1.6	0.7	-0.6	4.0	0.7	1.2	5.0
Other private[b]	3.1	4.7	4.7	4.0	3.6	2.9	2.7	3.0	4.0	3.7	3.3	5.0
TOTAL RESOURCE FLOWS (I+II+III)	**83.3**	**120.0**	**107.4**	**119.1**	**132.3**	**114.8**	**95.5**	**83.0**	**79.2**	**100.0**	**100.0**	**100.0**
For information:												
ODA grants	16.9	16.8	18.8	20.5	20.2	19.8	20.4	22.6	22.7	20.3	17.2	28.7
Private grants by NGOs	1.9	1.8	2.0	2.1	1.9	2.2	2.3	2.6	3.1	2.3	1.8	3.9
IMF purchases, net	-4.7	1.1	0.5	2.4	5.9	6.3	12.2	5.4	0.7	-5.6	2.0	0.9

[a] At 1984 prices and exchange rates.

[b] Including grants by non-governmental organizations (NGOs), shown for information below.

Source: OECD, Draft DAC Chairman's Report for 1986: Development Cooperation (DAC(86)46), September 5, 1986, Table III-1, p. III-2.

Components of U.S. Economic Assistance Program

The bilateral portion of U.S. economic aid is composed mainly of three programs: the Economic Support Fund (ESF), development assistance, and Public Law 480 food aid.

ESF, a descendant of the Marshall Plan defense support funds of the late 1940s, is the largest component. Its main purpose is "to provide budget support and development assistance to countries of political importance to the United States."[6] Most of the approximately $3 billion of economic support funds annually in recent years has been allocated to Israel, Egypt, and other countries of strategic importance, including those, such as Turkey and the Philippines, that provide access to military bases. African countries have also become important beneficiaries.

The influence of political and strategic interests in the allocation of bilateral economic aid is not confined to the United States. Of all French official development assistance, 30 percent is allocated to five small overseas departments and territories (Reunion, Martinique, Polynesia, New Caledonia, and Guadeloupe);[7] and 42 percent of concessional assistance from OPEC members provided through bilateral and OPEC-financed multilateral channels goes to two countries, Syria and Jordan.[8]

Although foreign policy considerations are dominant, the purpose of ESF assistance may include short-term stabilization as well as longer-term development. The kinds of activities financed vary from those with a substantial project orientation (as in Jordan and Pakistan) to straight balance-of-payments support (as in Israel). In short, ESF is the most flexible form of U.S. assistance and can be used to meet political, strategic, and economic interests or any combination of them.

Development assistance is the second-largest component, accounting for about 35 percent of total bilaterally distributed U.S. aid. In the 1960s, U.S. development programs concentrated on building physical infrastructure such as roads, dams, and power facilities in Third World countries. However, a shift in emphasis was mandated in 1973, when Congress required that development assistance be targeted to countries attempting to satisfy basic human needs and, within those countries, to the lower-income groups. The main concentration of expenditures in this category is for projects in agriculture and rural development; human resource programs, including nutrition, health, and education; and alternative energy development.

Development assistance was highly concentrated in the past, but it is now widely distributed. More than sixty countries receive some funding; and in many, the amounts are quite small. For example, although thirty-two developing countries received over $20 million each in U.S. bilateral assistance in 1981, the assistance accounted for more than 5 percent of imports in only ten cases.[9]

However small the amounts, aid provides a U.S. presence and a demonstration of U.S. concern in many countries, particularly in Africa, where development assistance is one of the few links we have. Nevertheless, the wide dispersion of aid raises the question of whether the amounts allocated to individual recipients are sufficient to form the basis of an effective policy dialogue. In our view, aid-financed programs are incomplete if they do not include explicit consideration of the country's overall policy environment because that environment inevitably has a large effect on the development impact of the assistance.

A further question is whether the mandated restraints on this category of assistance allow sufficient flexibility to ensure a long-run development impact. Stress on projects to ameliorate living conditions directly may in some cases carry the risk of having little long-term effect. Moreover, such projects commonly have a substantial recurrent local-cost component that can impose an unsustainable burden on a country's budget. Elimination of legislated restraints on program content would contribute to more effective development results.

Efforts to involve the recipient country's private sector have always been an element in U.S. aid programs. Under the Reagan Administration, greatly increased emphasis has been given to the promotion of private-sector initiatives. Concern has been expressed that this orientation may be incompatible with the objective of targeting development efforts to improving the lot of the poorest groups in developing countries. However, the two objectives are not in conflict.

> Private enterprises often can help meet basic needs in ways that over-extended public sectors cannot. For example, much of the private sector in developing countries consists of small-scale farmers or entrepreneurs who are themselves part of the poor majority. One area in which A.I.D. has apparently experienced considerable success is in creating or expanding intermediate financial institutions; the programs that make credit available to previously excluded groups can inject much-needed capital into small-scale farms and private enterprises.[10]

There is strong evidence that those countries that have given wide scope to market forces and private initiative have generally achieved the greatest success in development not only in terms of average per capita income but also when broader measures of social and economic welfare are taken into account. We therefore endorse AID's policies to energize the private sector as a means of encouraging broadly based, equitable, and self-sustaining economic growth and development. However, emphasis on private-sector initiatives should be seen, not as a substitute for, but rather as a complement of, official development assistance.

Food aid under P.L. 480 constitutes about one-quarter of bilaterally administered U.S. economic aid. When P.L. 480 was launched in 1954, its primary goals were the disposal of U.S. farm surpluses and the achievement of agricultural price stability; foreign economic development was a secondary objective. Since 1967, greater emphasis has been placed on its use to promote more effective agricultural and rural development policies as the best way to alleviate hunger and malnutrition in recipient countries. Nevertheless, establishing and maintaining markets for U.S. farm products remains an underlying concern of the program. Indeed, pressures are increasing to use food aid mainly as a way of disposing of surpluses.

Initially, P.L. 480 products were donated, bartered, or sold for local currency. As U.S. holdings of inconvertible foreign currencies grew, sales for dollars on concessional terms began. Today, the bulk of the food is sold for dollars on the basis of concessional loans, although sizable amounts continue to be donated for disaster relief and for nutritionally vulnerable groups such as young children and mothers. There is also a small program, about 15 percent of concessional sales, under which dollar repayment is waived in return for the investment of the local-currency equivalent in mutually agreed-upon agricultural projects designed to help the rural poor.

From the standpoint of the recipient country, P.L. 480 is a highly desirable type of resource transfer because in practice it is a flexible form of balance-of-payment and budget support. However, care must be taken in administering the programs to avoid adverse effects on local farm prices that would act as a disincentive to domestic agricultural producers.

General Issues in U.S. Economic Assistance

Two general issues pertaining to U.S. economic assistance merit attention: the size of the program and the question of the tying of assistance to purchases in the United States.

Size of the Program. Between 1981 and 1984, total U.S. official development assistance fluctuated around an average annual level of about $8 billion.[11] One way of assessing the adequacy of the U.S. contribution is to compare it with that of comparably affluent countries. The measure generally used for this purpose is the ratio of concessional assistance to the donor country's GNP.

In the late 1960s, the United Nations adopted an aid target of 0.7 percent of donor GNP. Some bilateral donors, notably the Scandinavian countries, have generally supported this target and have invoked it as a basis for expanding their assistance programs. Others have accepted it as a long-term goal; and still others, including the United States, have rejected it as politically unrealistic and economically unjustified.

Table 11 lists official development assistance disbursements by donor country along with the current performance of donors as measured by such assistance as a percentage of GNP. Norway, the Netherlands, and Sweden are at the top. The U.S. contribution of 0.24 percent of GNP is the lowest of all DAC countries and well below the average of 0.36 percent for the DAC countries.

If development assistance to the Third World is viewed as a common obligation of the community of more affluent industrial countries, it is not unreasonable that some practical principle of burden sharing should be followed. However, the United States has traditionally objected to the idea of a proportion of each donor country's GNP as a common target on the grounds that it fails to take into account other ways in which nations contribute to maintaining the international economic and political order in which they have a collective interest. In this connection, U.S. defense expenditures equivalent to 6 percent of GNP have been contrasted with the lower percentages for other DAC countries, particularly Japan, which falls below 1 percent.

Although there is substance to this line of reasoning, it is less a justification for declining U.S. contributions to international development assistance than an argument for drastic increases in Japan's contribution as compensation for the domestic political constraints on its defense expenditures. Although the trend in Japan's aid has been upward, it would not be unreasonable to expect Japan to increase its official development assistance several fold over the next few years and to channel it on an untied basis through multilateral development institutions.

A sharply stepped-up role for Japan in development assistance is consistent with the position advocated by Keizai Doyukai, CED's counterpart organization, in a recent policy statement.[12] Noting the weakness of "Japan's sense of responsibility and will to participate" in strengthening the international economic order, Keizai Doyukai calls upon Japan to "map out an effective strategy for comprehensive development cooperation." The program "should be aimed at expanding official development assistance, opening up the Japanese markets, promoting private direct investment and encouraging technology transfer."[13]

Insofar as U.S. assistance is concerned, it amounts to only one cent out of every budget dollar. We believe that contributions to official development assistance should at a minimum be maintained at the 1983–1984 level of 0.24 percent of GNP. This would imply a rise from $8.7 billion in 1984 to about $10 billion today. The $1.3-billion increase should be concentrated mainly on the development assistance component of the U.S. bilateral aid program but should also include this country's

Table 11

Official Development Assistance by DAC Countries
(dollars in millions)

Country	Amount 1984	As % of GNP 1983-1984 Average
Australia	$777	0.47%
Austria	181	0.26
Belgium	433	0.58
Canada	1,625	0.48
Denmark	449	0.79
Finland	178	0.34
France	3,788	0.75
Germany	2,782	0.47
Italy	1,133	0.28
Japan	4,319	0.34
Netherlands	1,268	0.96
New Zealand	55	0.26
Norway	543	1.06
Sweden	741	0.82
Switzerland	286	0.31
United Kingdom	1,418	0.34
United States	8,711	0.24
Total DAC countries	28,686	0.36

Source: OECD, Twenty-Five Years of Development Cooperation: 1985 Report, Statistical Annex, Table 1, p. 295.

share of enlarged funding for the IDA, the soft-loan window of the World Bank.

Much attention has been given to the problem of *aid fatigue* in the donor countries. However, this phenomenon is not pervasive. A number of countries have increased their aid programs substantially in recent years in the face of budgetary problems at least as serious as those of the United States.

However, the need for larger U.S. funding of official development assistance does not rest primarily on comparisons with other donor countries. Official development assistance plays a critical role in financing development in most low-income countries of Africa and Asia. In many of them, such assistance has amounted to more than 50 percent of total external financial receipts and has accounted for a substantial proportion of total investment and imports. For example, it recently equaled 31 percent of gross domestic investment in Bangladesh and 20 percent in Nepal. For those countries designated by the United Nations as *least developed,* official development assistance is equal to 10 percent of their GNP, 50 percent of their current imports, and 80 percent of their investment.[14]

The U.S. foreign aid program was recently reviewed by the bipartisian Commission on Security and Economic Assistance. In its report to the Secretary of State in November 1983, the commission concluded:

> The U.S. foreign cooperation program is inadequately funded. This judgment is not based upon the percentage of GNP contributed relative to other donors. Nor is it based on the Commission's observation that U.S. assistance levels—allowing for inflation—have fallen substantially in recent years. The judgment rests upon the need for resources to maintain our leadership role and meet our foreign policy objectives . . . political, economic, strategic and humanitarian.[15]

Aid Tying. Requiring the recipient to spend economic assistance funds in the donor country is one of the principal mechanisms used by donors to promote their commercial interests through their aid programs. Virtually all donors resort to source tying to some extent in their bilateral assistance. In 1982, some 60 percent of U.S. bilateral loans and 25 percent of bilateral grants were tied.[16]

Tying reduces the effectiveness of any given volume of aid. By restricting the source, the goods and services procured with tied aid may cost more, be of lower quality, and be less appropriate to the recipient's specific needs. Studies of the costs of aid tying have generally estimated the reduction in the value of development loans resulting from this practice at about 15 to 20 percent, although the costs associated with individual aid transactions may far exceed these levels. The excess costs are, in effect, subsidies to the donor country's exporters.

However, tying creates a business constituency for aid at a time when general public support for the program is weak. Untying aid might well entail a price in terms of a lower volume of aid.

The practice of tying is especially prevalent in bilateral loans (as opposed to grants). In the case of tied loans, the borrower is required to pay interest and repay principal not only on the true value of the loan but also on the excess value representing the implicit subsidy to the exporter. It would seem only fair to relieve the aid recipient of the burden of this excess interest and principal repayment obligation.

Mixed Credits. In recent years, donors have resorted increasingly to tying through mixed credits. This practice involves the use of concessional assistance in combination with public or publicly guaranteed export credits to produce credit terms considerably softer than those of market loans. Typically, the entire financing package is tied to procurement in the donor country.

Until the late 1970s, mixed credits were a comparatively minor element in total concessional assistance or export credit programs of donor countries. A major exception was the French program, in which mixed credits were a standard aid mechanism. Between 1981 and 1984, however, a total of $12.7 billion in "associated financing" transactions was reported to DAC by fifteen donor countries.[17] To support these transactions, $4.4 billion of official development assistance was allocated. France has been by far the principal user of this technique, accounting for 52 percent of all DAC-associated financing in 1983 and 1984, followed by Canada with 14 percent and the United Kingdom with 11 percent.

Because the principal goal of mixed credits is to gain a commercial advantage in exporting, they have been severely criticized on the grounds that they undermine the effectiveness of development assistance and unfairly distort international trade. From a development standpoint, it is argued that mixed credits bias aid allocations away from low-income countries and priority activities with a low import content, such as rural development, in favor of capital-intensive projects, such as transport and power, that involved heavy outlays for imported equipment. On the other hand, supporters of mixed credits argue that this instrument contributes to development by stretching scarce official development assistance and by improving the quality of export credits by involving the judgment and monitoring of aid agencies. It is also claimed that mixed credits are appropriate for middle-income countries, where the major use of official development assistance is no longer justified but where some continuing access to concessional resources is nevertheless warranted.

Whatever the net effect of mixed credits from the perspective of development, they are an undesirable practice from the standpoint of commercial policy. By creating an artificial and unfair advantage for their user, they distort international trade at a time of keen competition for export markets. Moreover, the practice tends to spread. Many countries have stated to the OECD that they are introducing associated financing in order to enable their exporters to have access to credit on terms no less favorable than those enjoyed by their competitors. As a defensive measure, Congress authorized AID in 1983 to finance mixed credits in cooperation with the Export-Import Bank.[18]

The defensive adoption of mixed credits is clearly a second-best response to the distortions they induce. Much preferable would be an international agreement to eliminate mixed credits entirely, and we believe the United States should persist in its efforts toward that end. In the meantime, AID and the Export-Import Bank should continue to be endowed with the authority to match the credit terms offered by others while this country supports OECD efforts to reach agreement on principles that would reduce the use of mixed credits and minimize their adverse effects.[19]

Multilateral Development Assistance

Approximately one-quarter of official development assistance is conveyed through multilateral rather than bilateral channels. This proportion holds not only for the United States but also for all DAC countries as a group. The principal vehicles for multilateral assistance are the World Bank group and the regional development banks (see "Systems of Multilateral Development Institutions").

Bilateral Versus Multilateral Assistance

Multilateral assistance has come under increasing attack in the United States in recent years. The basic argument is that the case for foreign aid is inherently political and that bilateral assistance, over which the donor has greater control and with which the donor is directly identified, is a superior instrument for meeting political objectives.

There is little doubt about the advantage of bilateral assistance in serving U.S. *short-term* political and strategic interests. Complete donor control of the funding provides a flexible instrument for supporting particular regimes and influencing their policies and for serving as a visible sign of U.S. commitment to them. It also provides a mechanism for pursuing U.S. short-term economic interests through policies such as aid tying and mixed credits. Of the various forms of U.S. bilateral

Systems of Multilateral Development Institutions

The World Bank is the largest of the multilateral development banks and consists formally of three components: the International Bank for Reconstruction and Development (IBRD), which lends to developing countries at market-related terms; the IDA, which lends at highly concessional terms; and the IFC, which helps to mobilize domestic and foreign private capital to stimulate the growth of the private sector in developing countries.

Regional banks (Asian, African, and Inter-American) provide financing to developing countries within their respective regions. To a considerable extent, they are staffed with nationals of countries in the region. The regional banks and the World Bank share the common objective of promoting economic growth and social development in the developing world.

Typically, the institutions have capital and concessional lending windows. Finance for the capital windows comes largely from borrowings on world capital markets against pledges of callable capital by donor countries. Terms of loans from capital windows are usually somewhat better than obtainable by the most creditworthy developing countries in international capital markets. Concessional windows obtain their resources almost entirely from direct budgetary contributions of donors and lend to low-income countries on highly concessional terms.

In addition to the multilateral development banks, there is the United Nations Development Program (UNDP), which is the major multilateral instrument for providing technical assistance to the developing world on a grant basis. Operating through the specialized agencies and other United Nations bodies, the UNDP provides a coordinating focus for the technical assistance efforts of various UN agencies, including the Food and Agriculture Organization, the World Health Organization, and the United Nations International Children's Emergency Fund (UNICEF).

assistance, the ESF, with its fast-disbursing capability, is the most flexible vehicle for supporting these short-term interests. U.S. bilateral aid can also be cut off more rapidly than multilateral aid in response to political concerns.

When it comes to the *longer-term* objective of a secure and prosperous world consonant with U.S. political and security interests, multilateral development assistance possesses some decided advantages. To a much greater extent than bilateral aid, multilateral concessional assistance is allocated to low-income countries.[20] Many of these are countries in which interests may be of secondary importance today but which, in the absence of economic and social progress, could become the focal point of future instability and conflict involving the major powers directly or indirectly. Moreover, the multilateral channel serves U.S. long-term global political interests by supporting economic development programs in countries where bilateral relations may be politically sensitive (e.g., Zimbabwe and Yugoslavia).

Another advantage of the multilateral channel is budgetary. It enables the United States to pursue its objectives at a lower cost to the American taxpayer than if an equivalent volume of funds was appropriated by the U.S. itself. Because the United States' contribution to the multilateral development banks averages about 25 percent of the total, other countries provide $3 for every U.S. dollar. This resource leveraging is even greater in the hard-loan windows, where only 10 percent or less of the U.S. contribution is paid in and involves budgetary outlays. Because the rest of the funds are mobilized from other donors and private capital markets, a dollar of U.S. budgetary outlays supports at least 40 times as much development assistance in the form of loans through the ordinary capital windows.

Both bilateral and multilateral assistance share the aim of promoting Third World economic development within the framework of an open, interdependent, and expanding world economy. Encouraging countries to move away from highly interventionist government policies toward more liberal economic regimes has proved to be an important element in stimulating development. In general, the multilateral development banks are better placed than bilateral donors to provide economic advice and to influence the developing countries toward market-directed changes in policies. This superiority derives from the larger scale of their assistance, the recipients' perception of their impartiality and the fact that the recipients are members of the banks and therefore have a voice in determining their policies.

It is clear that both multilateral and bilateral assistance serve important U.S. objectives. The two should be regarded, not as substitutes for each other, but as complements, each with its own comparative advantage. As summed up by the U.S. Treasury:

> The U.S. bilateral aid program can often move more quickly to support U.S. short-term political interests and priority countries, and also stimulates LDC growth by bringing to bear U.S. expertise on key development constraints in recipient countries; multilateral assistance primarily serves long-term U.S. interests, can be very cost effective, and promotes a stable international economic environment.[21]

In light of the constructive role of the multilateral development banks, we had viewed with concern the early policy of the Reagan Administration to move toward "greater emphasis on bilateral aid."[22] We welcome the recent indications by Treasury Secretary James Baker of the return to a more balanced approach. Particularly encouraging was Baker's statement at the 1985 meeting of the IMF and World Bank to the effect that the United States would be prepared to seriously consider the timing and scope of a general capital increase for the World Bank as the demand for its loans increases.

International Development Association

IDA is the soft-loan window of the World Bank. It gives the Bank the flexibility to assist many of the poorer countries that are not in a position to service hard loans and to blend the terms of its hard and soft loans in proportions that are appropriate to individual borrowing countries.

For some time now, the United States has exerted downward pressure on the scale of IDA activities. In the sixth replenishment of IDA, the U.S. commitment, which had been budgeted by the Carter Administration at about $1 billion a year, was effectively reduced by stretching out the payments over five fiscal years instead of three. In that period, other donor countries increased their payments, partially making up the U.S. shortfall.

For the seventh replenishment of IDA, which is currently being funded, former World Bank President A. W. Clausen and most of the donor governments urged a minimum commitment of $12 billion over the three-year period. However, the United States insisted that a $9-billion program was the largest total to which it would agree. Based on a 25 percent share of the total, that meant a $2.25-billion commitment amounting to an annual contribution of $750 million over three years.[23]

There are indications, however, of a more positive U.S. attitude toward IDA. In January 1986, donor countries including the United States agreed to work toward an enlarged eighth replenishment. Negotiations for the funding are well under way.

IDA is the single largest source of concessional assistance for the world's poorest countries. Because of its limited funds and the softness of its terms,[24] IDA lends only to countries with an annual average per capita income of $790 or less. About 80 percent of its cumulative commitments and well over 90 percent of its current program have gone to countries with per capita incomes of $400 or less. (U.S. per capita income was over $15,000 in 1984.) In accordance with its Articles of Agreement, IDA is prohibited from lending to a country that can obtain financing "from private sources on terms which are reasonable for the recipient or could be provided by a loan of the type made by the Bank."[25]

Despite their high concessionality, IDA loans are not charity. They must meet all the criterion for economic, financial, and technical soundness that apply to other World Bank loans. These standards have resulted in average rates of return of 17 percent, compared with 19 percent for other World Bank projects.

The high rate of return on IDA projects has led some observers to question the necessity of this form of development assistance. However, the long-term nature of the returns on IDA projects makes nonconcessional financing infeasible. Often, benefits cannot readily be turned directly into foreign exchange to meet debt-service requirements.

Another measure of IDA success is the twenty-eight countries that have graduated to other sources of financing. They include the Republic of Korea, Turkey, Tunisia, and Nigeria. Only seven of the recipients of the initial allocation of IDA credits in 1960–1964 are still borrowers.

Despite the record of graduation from IDA lending, the need for concessional aid among the remaining low-income countries has increased. These countries were hard hit by the oil price increases in the 1970s and the worldwide recession of the 1980s. The terms of trade of the low-income African countries deteriorated sharply in the early 1980s, and this downward trend is continuing. Although the decline in world oil prices provides some relief, the poorest countries will remain heavily dependent on international aid for their basic development for some time to come.

We therefore welcome the change in the U.S. Administration's attitude toward IDA and recommend that, in the future, it take the lead in supporting IDA replenishment on a significantly larger scale than in the past.

Project Versus Program Lending

Development assistance implies supplementing domestic savings with a transfer of resources from abroad. How should those resources be transferred? They may be transferred through *project loans* (i.e., funds earmarked for the importation of capital goods for specific projects) or through program loans (i.e., funds used for importing goods and services not earmarked for particular projects but intended to support a development program as a whole). Program lending is sometimes referred to as *general balance-of-payments support* or *nonproject lending*.

The question of project versus program lending is applicable to the operations of all development assistance organizations, bilateral and multilateral. Most donors show a strong preference for project financing, with its tangible and identifiable increases in productive capacity, rather than program assistance, where the imports financed cannot be precisely traced through to final output. In a number of areas, however, the preference for project assistance has resulted in a proliferation of projects that has strained the financial and human capacity of low-income countries to monitor and maintain them and to utilize their capacity fully.[26]

The issue arises with particular force in the case of the World Bank. The traditional role of that organization has been as a project lender with impressive strengths in project design, supervision, and management. Although the Bank has over the years done a modest amount of program lending, (e.g., the IDA industrial import credits for India and Pakistan in the late 1960s), it has historically felt constrained from departing very far from project lending. Nevertheless, its conception of project lending has pragmatically widened over the years from heavy concentration on basic infrastructure such as specific power and transport projects to broader sector loans encompassing packages of related activities in fields such as agriculture and rural development, education, and energy as well as credits to industrial development banks enabling them in turn to lend to private firms for a wide range of productive purposes.

Two principal arguments have been advanced in favor of a larger scope for nonproject lending. The first is related to the proliferation of projects in low-income countries. In some countries, the shortage of resources for development may not take the form of inadequate productive capacity to be met through traditional project lending. Rather it is reflected in an inability to utilize *existing* capacity effectively because an insufficiency of foreign exchange makes it impossible to import the necessary raw materials, intermediate products, or spare parts. In such a case, nonproject lending would be more appropriate because it would relieve the foreign exchange constraint.

The second argument is not unrelated to the first. It is that severe balance-of-payment problems, often reflected in idle human and physical capacity, are commonly due to structural maladjustments in the economy as a whole that can be overcome only through fundamental changes in policy. In such cases, program or balance-of-payments assistance is commonly regarded as a more effective vehicle for encouraging and supporting basic policy reform than lending that is narrowly targeted to specific projects. In project lending, the aid-giving agency normally deals with officials from technical departments such as transport or power, where responsibilities are narrowly focused. But program assistance involves ministries of economics and finance and therefore lends itself more effectively to a broad policy dialogue between donors and recipients.

In response to the severe economic shocks of the 1970s and the growing debt-servicing problems of the developing countries, the World Bank in 1980 initiated an articulated program of nonproject lending in the form of structural adjustment loans. In contrast with project loans that are paid out over a period of years, structural adjustment loans (SALs) are characterized by rapid disbursement. They are intended to support specific policy changes and institutional reforms and to assist a country in meeting the transitional costs of structural changes by augmenting the supply of freely usable foreign exchange. The major types of reforms supported by structural adjustment loans are changes in trade regimes to improve the competitiveness of, and incentives for, exports;

improvements in internal resource mobilization through changes in budget and interest rate policy; improvements in pricing policies in agriculture and energy as well as incentive systems in industry; and institutional reforms in such fields as tax administration, public-sector investment management, debt-management systems and civil service organization.

The World Bank also extends nonproject assistance through *sector adjustment loans.* These operations are designed to support comprehensive policy changes and institutional reforms in a specific sector in countries where circumstances, such as limited implementation capability, would not permit a broader structural adjustment loan to be carried out effectively. Together, structural and sector adjustment loans amounted to about $3.1 billion in fiscal 1986, or 18 percent of total World Bank lending, including lending by the African Facility.

We recognize that the main purpose of development assistance is to improve the efficiency with which a recipient country uses its total resources rather than simply to add to and monitor closely the margin of additional resources, which for any individual donor is likely to be small in percentage terms. It follows, therefore, that donor agencies, including the World Bank, should have considerable flexibility to transfer funds in a manner that is most effective in improving the general economic policy framework of recipient countries and in catalyzing the mobilization of their domestic resources.

At the same time, we recognize the special strengths of the World Bank as a project-lending institution and the considerable scope that its traditional project operations afford for influencing policy in particular fields and for working with private institutions to stretch its own resources. On balance, therefore, we believe that the Bank should have the discretion to expand its total nonproject lending beyond the present 15 to 20 percent of its total lending. These increases should be limited, however, to levels that would not jeopardize the Bank's ability to raise funds in the private capital markets.

Strong conditionality of lending by the multilateral development banks and the IMF is in the interest of both borrowers and lenders, whether public or private. Capital is a scarce resource. Unless it is used wisely, the returns will be inadequate to stimulate growth in the developing countries while permitting external debt to be serviced through increases in export earnings. Unrealistic exchange rates, price distortions, protection, and subsidies all militate against the achievement of efficient and internationally competitive industries. We therefore strongly endorse policy conditionality by the development banks and the IMF and regard it as the key to unlocking a significantly larger flow of private credit to the developing countries.

Relations Between the World Bank and the IMF

The World Bank's move toward balance-of-payments lending through its structural adjustment loan program sharpens the whole question of the relationship between the two Bretton Woods organizations, the Bank and the IMF. Traditionally, the distinction between the two was seen in the focus of the Bank on long-term economic development and the IMF on short-term balance-of-payments financing and adjustment. However, in 1974, the IMF created the Extended Fund Facility (EFF), which moved it toward the longer-term lending of the Bank. For loans under the EFF, the IMF lengthened the repayment schedule from the standard three to five years to ten years. Also suggestive of a shift toward the Bank's domain was the statement that the EFF's purpose was to assist members suffering from "slow growth and an inherently weak balance-of-payments position which prevents pursuit of an active development policy."[27]

The establishment of the EFF by the IMF and the later inauguration of structural adjustment lending by the Bank "involved each institution in a kind of lending that had previously been considered the primary responsibility of the other."[28] True, the distinction between development lending and balance-of-payments finance has never been precise, but the difference in the emphases of the two organizations has become more blurred than ever.[29]

Traditionally, the IMF has focused primarily on balance-of-payments problems that were reversible in the short run. The corrective measures have been mainly macroeconomic, consisting largely of policies affecting aggregate demand and overall relative price levels (i.e., fiscal, monetary, and exchange rate policies). With the help of short-term financial support, such measures could be effective over a span of two or three years in restoring equilibrium in a country's payments position.

In contrast, the Bank has focused primarily on supply, i.e., the long-run augmentation of a country's productive resources and improvements in the effectiveness of their use. The traditional vehicle for assistance has been long-term project loans, and much of the Bank's policy guidance has related to microeconomic matters such as the pricing of the services of public enterprises, incentive systems, and trade policy.

The policy conditionality of Bank and IMF lending has typically entailed politically difficult economic reforms in recipient countries. But there is a difference between the two. Because IMF conditionality has related largely to macroeconomic measures (e.g., changes in the money supply, total government expenditures and revenues, and the exchange rate), it has tended to affect all classes and groups in society. However unpleasant, the measures are generally accepted as an inevitable national sacrifice that may before long yield tangible economic improvement for the country as a whole. Policy reforms sought by the Bank, on the other hand, have related more to changes in the *structure* of government expenditures, taxation, and incentives. They tend, therefore, to entail disproportionate costs for particular interest groups, such as beneficiaries of import protection or recipients of special government subsidies. As is well known, the likelihood of organized resistance and effective political opposition is greater when reforms are targeted to particular and identifiable interest groups.

Increasingly, however, the dichotomy between the roles of the two institutions has become artificial and unsustainable. For many developing countries, the two oil price shocks and the worldwide recession demonstrated that severe balance-of-payments problems could be exogenous in origin and could not always be corrected through the compression of demand within the standard time frame of traditional IMF lending. The IMF is therefore increasingly taking into account supply as well as demand management considerations, and many of its programs necessarily have a medium-term perspective. For its part, the Bank is acutely aware that effective long-term development programs cannot be carried out by a country disrupted by financial crisis. In such cases, stabilization measures, supported by IMF assistance, are often needed as a foundation for a program of structural adjustment lending. In short, "the Bank's SALs and the IMF programs are in practice complementary and mutually reinforcing."[30]

Given the overlapping range of World Bank and IMF concerns with stabilization and growth policies, closer cooperation between the two institutions is essential. Recognition of their commonality of interest is formally reflected in the requirement that members of the Bank be members of the IMF and in the establishment in 1974 of the Development Committee composed of the board of governors of both institutions. Beyond the formalities, however, it is necessary to foster continuous collaboration at the working level and compatible financing in order to ensure that the responsibilities of each institution are exercised with due regard for the interests of the other. Toward that end, we endorse the recommendation made more than fifteen years ago by the Pearson Commission that "the World Bank and the IMF, in countries where both operate, should adopt procedures for preparing unified country assessments and assuring consistent policy advice."[31]

Official Finance and the Private Sector

Both bilateral and multilateral aid agencies are placing increased emphasis on enhancing the role of the private sector in promoting growth and development in the Third World. This objective is being pursued by official agencies in two ways: (1) by encouraging the liberalization of markets through policy and institutional reform in the developing countries and (2) by enlisting the collaboration of private capital, both domestic and foreign, in joint financing arrangements with official lenders.

Policy and Institutional Reform

Although private enterprise has been the most dynamic element in those countries that have achieved rapid economic growth, the private sector still faces major impediments in much of the developing world. Those impediments reflect ingrained attitudes, institutional deficiencies, and interventionist government policies.

Hostility to private enterprise and the profit motive is in many cases a carryover of experience from the colonial period, when large foreign trading and mining companies often dominated the economies of Third World countries. With the coming of independence, there was a tendency to look to the newly formed governments to control and direct the local economy and to undertake many of the basic productive functions formerly carried out by colonial enterprises. Little attention was given, therefore, to the need to create conditions favorable to the emergence of new private firms, especially indigenous financial institutions to provide credit to the private sector. Even in the bilateral and multilateral assistance agencies, "the thrust of the development effort has been directed toward public sector activities" over the past two or three decades.[32]

In recent years, a shift in emphasis has occurred. Official development agencies are now giving high priority to establishing conditions that will encourage strong and vigorous private sectors in developing countries, including capital markets. Improvements are being encouraged in banking and credit facilities accessible not only to large firms but to smaller entrepreneurs as well. Other areas of reform include legal and accounting services, management training, and for the agricultural sector, extension services, crop insurance, and more secure land tenure systems.

In addition to supporting institutional reforms, development assistance agencies are encouraging the liberalization of domestic markets. Price and wage controls, trade restrictions, inappropriate subsidies, interest rate ceilings, overvalued exchange rates, and similar forms of government intervention and market distortions have been all too prevalent in the Third World. Often they result in conditions leading to capital flight that offsets the inflows of development assistance from abroad. Fortunately, the developing countries themselves have recognized the adverse effects of comprehensive systems of control, and they have been encouraged and supported by both bilateral and multilateral assistance organizations in granting wider scope to market forces.

We believe the private sector has a unique and vital role to play in the development process and therefore strongly endorse programs of institution building and policy reform that help to release the forces of private initiative and entrepreneurship.

Cofinancing

Cofinancing with private lenders is another way in which official aid agencies enlist the support of the private sector for Third World development. From the perspective of the official agency, cofinancing is a means of stretching limited aid funds. From the perspective of the borrowers, cofinancing often provides longer maturities and better terms than strictly private loans. It may also open access to the private market for countries that would otherwise not be deemed creditworthy. From the perspective of the private lenders, cofinancing with an official development agency generally provides a less risky investment than lending on its own. The official agency provides information on the borrowing country that may not be accessible to the private lender. It is also generally in a better position to assess the economic soundness of the project to be financed and to speak effectively against policies in borrower countries that undermine the repayability of the credit. As risk aversion becomes a more prominent feature of private bank lending to developing countries, cofinancing should become a more attractive way of lending.

The World Bank cofinances more projects than any other development institution. Between 1977 and 1986, it cofinanced 106 projects with private lenders for a total of about $8.4 billion. Until 1983, loans from the Bank and private sources for a particular cofinanced project were separate, although some were linked by an optional cross-default clause. The clause allows either lender to suspend disbursement on the loan or accelerate repayment if the other party does so for good cause. However, neither party is obligated to take action following action by the other. As a matter of policy, the World Bank will not accept a mandatory cross-default obligation.

In 1983, the World Bank introduced on a trial basis a set of new cofinancing instruments that provide for a closer linking of its lending with that of private providers. Under this new program, the Bank, in addition to making its own loan for a project, may participate in the parallel commercial loan. This could consist of the Bank taking the later maturities of a loan by commercial banks, the use of the Bank guarantee for the later maturities, or a contingent participation in the final maturity of a floating-rate loan.[33] Market placements under the new program for the 1984–1986 period were close to $2 billion and have involved 280 banks. The World Bank's share was about $240 million, implying a leverage of eight to one.

Although the U.S. government has supported the new cofinancing arrangements, it has not favored their use in concerted *involuntary* lending by the commercial banks. For example, the United States objected to World Bank cofinancing in such a new money package for Chile. However, it has supported the use of the new instruments in voluntary lending for projects in the productive sector of the Chilean economy.

The new cofinancing instruments are a promising innovation for voluntary lending. Because of the World Bank's direct stake in the commercial loan, the new program offers greater assurance to the private lender. At the same time, it encourages an extension of maturities of commercial loans to lengths more appropriate to the development nature of the investments and to the borrowers' ability to pay.

The World Bank has not limited its cofinancing to the commercial banks. Export credit agencies have also been major participants, with placements averaging $863 million in 1985 and 1986. The Bank's participation in these cofinancings can help make the provision of export financing more consistent with development objectives.

Unlike the World Bank, its affiliate, the *IFC* has been involved in cofinancing since its inception in 1956. The mission of the IFC is to stimulate the growth of private investment in developing countries by promoting and participating in the financing of profitable projects for which adequate capital is not available from other sources on reasonable terms.[34]

All IFC loans and equity investments are cofinanced with domestic or foreign partners, reflecting its aim to mobilize and supplement private capital rather than substitute for it. In addition to investing capital, the IFC provides technical assistance (legal, financial, and engineering) and helps the partners in a project arrive at mutually satisfactory arrangements. Through fiscal 1986, the IFC participated in 933 projects with a total cost of $33 billion. In recent years, it has increased its role in the low-income countries, with a particular emphasis on sub-Saharan Africa. To support the expansion and diversification of the IFC's activities, its board has recommended that its authorized capital be doubled from $650 million to $1.3 billion. We urge Congress to approve this increase.

AID also engages in cofinancing on a small scale through its Bureau for Private Enterprise. It has cofinanced with private commercial lenders in both the United States and the developing world and with the IFC. The projects that AID has cofinanced have been concentrated in ten countries chosen for strategic as well as economic reasons.

In supporting programs of development assistance, the United States should promote the increased use of cofinancing wherever feasible. In particular, we endorse the closer links with private financial institutions made possible by the World Bank's new instruments for participating in the later maturities of private loans. In this regard, we believe the Bank's Articles of Agreement should be amended so that a Bank guarantee of a private loan would count somewhat less than one for one against its capital, thereby reducing its own lending capacity by less than the full amount of the guarantee.

Although most cofinancing is for projects in middle-income developing countries, it also helps poorer countries by freeing official resources for use there. Nevertheless, cofinancing should not be regarded as a substitute for other means of development finance. It is best seen primarily as an aid for investment in middle-income countries and as a means to provide the lower-income countries with an increase in official funds on a concessional basis.

Aid Coordination

Given the multiplicity of bilateral and multilateral aid agencies, the need for effective coordination to ensure consistent and mutually reinforcing policies has long been recognized.

From the U.S. standpoint, however, the highest priority is to achieve effective coordination among the many domestic agencies with an interest in foreign aid, especially the AID, the Export-Import Bank, and the Departments of State, Defense, Treasury, and Agriculture. Each of these agencies has its own constituency and perspective and in most cases controls a share of the budget for development assistance. On the basis of past experience, we conclude that a coordinating center is required and that it should have strong Presidential support.

For the multilateral coordination of aid, the DAC was established in 1961 by the major industrial country aid donors of the OECD. The DAC collects, analyzes, exchanges, and disseminates information on the assistance programs and policies of its members. Regular meetings are held to discuss development issues and to formulate general aid principles.

The World Bank has been and should remain the key donor agency in coordinating aid policies and programs. It is the sponsor of consultative groups in nearly thirty developing countries. These groups, which are composed of both donors and recipients, meet at one- or two-year intervals to review the World Bank economic analysis of the recipient country, the development plan of the recipient country, and the donor's current and prospective aid programs. The consultative groups often represent the only mechanism for bringing donors and recipients together to discuss development problems and programs.

In recent years, increased efforts have been made to achieve better coordination of aid programs at the international level. The UNDP has become more actively involved in country-level coordination through its round tables. Groups such as the Club du Sahel, the Central American Consultative Group, and the Consultative Group on International Agricultural Research have been established to harmonize aid policies in particular regions and sectors. There has also been an increase in coordination and cofinancing between multilateral development banks and bilateral official development agencies.

Most recently, attention has been focused on in-country aid coordination. Both the DAC and the World Bank issued reports in 1984 calling for an increase in aid coordination with particular attention to "on-the-ground" efforts. The World Bank has encouraged the consultative groups to hold more frequent meetings in recipient countries to concentrate on problems in carrying out aid programs. In an effort to assist in the in-country coordination, the World Bank has increased its resident missions, giving particular attention to the sub-Saharan-African countries. In the final analysis, true coordination must be carried out in the recipient country.

Better aid coordination should be encouraged as one way to stretch the aid dollar. It provides advantages for both donor and recipient by pooling resources, ensuring greater complementarity, and tailoring projects more effectively to the development needs and priorities of the recipient countries.

5

Foreign Private Investment

The stagnation of the volume of official development assistance and the contraction of voluntary bank lending to developing countries have highlighted the question of how the continuing external financial needs of the developing countries can be met. In this context, increasing attention is being given to the possibilities for augmenting other flows of foreign capital, primarily direct investment but also portfolio equity investment. The Baker initiative, announced on October 8, 1985, emphasized the vital role that foreign private investment can play as part of a comprehensive program to restore healthy economic growth in the Third World.[1]

Direct investment is defined as flows of capital from a parent company to a foreign affiliate. It can include new equity capital, reinvested earnings, or net lending by the parent to the affiliate. The distinguishing characteristic of direct investment is the acquisition of a lasting interest and an effective voice in the management of a foreign enterprise.

In contrast, *portfolio equity investment* consists of the acquisition of a share of ownership without an effective influence in the policies or management of an enterprise. Portfolio equity capital has not been important as a source of external finance for developing countries in recent years, but it may have significant potential in the future.

Attitudes Toward Direct Investment

Foreign direct investment has been regarded with deep suspicion in much of the developing world. Fear of economic exploitation and political domination by powerful multinational corporations has colored attitudes and has conditioned host-country policies and regulations. As a result, severely restrictive conditions often face the foreign investor.

In some developing countries, however, a greater receptivity to foreign investment has emerged. This change reflects an intellectual reassessment of the threats posed by foreign companies as well as the benefits they offer and the maturation of countries, many of which achieved independence only after the Second World War. These countries have now gained greater confidence in their ability to assert their sovereign authority and to exercise stronger bargaining power in their dealings with foreign companies.

Most important, however, has been the impact of the debt crisis and the austerity measures required in conjunction with debt restructuring. A comment by the finance minister of Ecuador sums it up: "We feel that it is better to have partners than creditors. I can say that with full authority, having just refinanced our foreign debt."[2] But for this change in attitude to induce a larger flow of foreign capital, it will have to be reflected in actual improvements in the investment climate, including the laws, regulations, and administrative practices applying to foreign enterprise.

Special Characteristics of Direct Investment

Unlike private bank lending, direct foreign investment does not consist simply of a flow of finance. One of the advantages for developing countries is that along with capital, direct investment typically provides a unique package of other resources, including technology, know-how, management, training, and facilities for marketing the product or service. Because the recorded volume of direct investment does not reflect the flow of these nonfinancial resources, it normally significantly understates the importance of this type of capital to the host country.

Another advantage of direct investment compared with bank lending is its greater stability as an element of resource flows. Although direct investment increased much less rapidly than commercial lending over the past decade, its volume has tended to hold up better during periods of crisis. Direct investment does tend to decline during periods of economic adversity, but not to the extent of the contraction of commercial lending during the recent recession and debt-servicing difficulties.

In recent years, much of private bank lending to developing countries has consisted of short-term loans that were used to finance long-term investments. When a country's external financial position deteriorates, banks are reluctant to roll the loans over. In contrast, direct investment is by nature a long-term commitment and therefore more in line with the maturity structure of the underlying investments (although some direct investors may seek to recoup their equity in a few years).

The two forms of private finance also differ with respect to the distribution of risk between the provider and the recipient. Both commercial lenders and foreign investors are exposed to the balance-of-payments risk if a recipient country becomes unable to provide the foreign exchange with which to service a loan or remit the earnings on a direct investment. However, income payments on foreign investment tend to correlate more closely with a country's ability to service them than do interest payments on external debt. Profit remittances are not a set amount; they depend on the commercial success of the foreign venture. But interest payments continue even if the original loan financed unprofitable investments. In short, although both types of foreign capital involve a balance-of-payments risk, the project risk is borne by the provider of capital in the case of direct investment but by the recipient of the capital in the case of commercial loans.[3] Some caution is in order in drawing sharp distinctions between risk elements in foreign direct investment and commercial lending. Subsidiaries of transnational corporations have been substantial borrowers in international financial markets, although such flows are not included in the data on direct investment. To the extent that the proportion of such debt is large compared with the equity of foreign affiliates, the distinctions between the locus of risk in the two forms of financing would need to be modified.[4]

Nevertheless, the debt crisis struck a blow to the conventional wisdom that commercial borrowing had the advantage of providing unencumbered resources, whereas direct investment by definition implied at least some degree of foreign control over the operations of local enterprises. Developing countries discovered that in the end, borrowing resulted in more, not less, external intervention. When debt-repayment schedules could not be met, countries had no effective alternative but to submit to severe austerity programs as the condition for debt rescheduling and IMF emergency financing. The alleged problems associated with foreign control over this or that local enterprise receded in the wake of the far-reaching economic, social, and political consequences of externally negotiated conditionality.

Types of Direct Investment

Broadly speaking direct foreign investment in the Third World is undertaken for one of three reasons: to develop and export minerals or other natural resources; to manufacture products or produce services for sale in the local market; or to establish a base for the export of manufactured products to the home- or third-country markets. Although the three are not entirely distinct, it is useful to differentiate them for analytical purposes (see "Three Models of Direct Investment").

Three Models of Direct Investment

Resource Investment

The classical pattern of direct investment in Third World countries has consisted of the establishment of a subsidiary, typically wholly owned by the parent company, to develop and extract minerals for processing at home within an integrated operation or for export to third parties. Because little processing normally took place in the developing country, mining operations were regarded as *enclave* investments with few links to the local economy and therefore yielding only limited developmental benefits. In recent years, however, host governments have encouraged or required some local processing (e.g., the many refineries that have been set up in oil-producing developing countries).

As raw material prices soared in the early and mid-1970s, a number of developing countries sought a greater degree of control over their natural resources, especially oil and copper. Local private or state-owned companies and joint ventures were favored over wholly owned foreign subsidiaries. In some cases, existing foreign enterprises were nationalized, and restrictions were placed on new investments. Typically, the classical model of equity ownership gave way to new contractual arrangements in which the multinational firm continued to provide organizational, technological, and marketing services in return for a fee or a share of the output.

Beginning in the latter half of the 1970s, foreign investment in nonfuel minerals slowed down worldwide because of excess capacity and sagging relative prices. Exploration activities stagnated or declined, particularly in developing countries. Adverse market prospects were compounded in the Third World by concerns about the security of foreign investment as affected by the changing relations between mining companies and host governments.

Investment for the Local Market

Investment in manufacturing aimed mainly at local markets may be undertaken for any of a number of reasons. Often, such investment has been induced by trade barriers imposed in the context of import-substitution strategies of industrialization. As the trade restrictions effectively precluded the continuation of exports from the parent company's home base, the only way to preserve market share was to establish an affiliate to produce locally.

Other motivations have included the desire to improve the ability to serve a foreign market by developing, through local manufacturing, better relations with distributors, superior service to customers, increased opportunities to utilize local materials and design products specifically for the local market, and lower transportation costs. Naturally, the attractiveness of producing abroad for local sale is enhanced to the extent that the host-country market is large and growing rapidly.

Much of foreign direct investment in manufacturing in Latin America has been undertaken primarily to serve rapidly growing and protected domestic markets. For example, majority-owned manufacturing affiliates of U.S. companies in Latin America exported only 6 percent of their total sales during the 1966–1976 period. In contrast, U.S. affiliates in Asia had exports amounting to 24 percent of total sales. In recent years, however, the contrast between the two regions has become less sharp as Latin American countries have been shifting from import-substitution to greater emphasis on export orientation in conjunction with structural adjustment programs.[a]

[a]OECD, "Foreign Investment in Developing Countries," unpublished note by the Secretariat, 11 October 1984, p. 8.

(*continues*)

Three Models of Direct Investment, continued

A growing proportion of the direct investment primarily for the domestic market has been in the service sector, especially banking, insurance, trade, and advertising. To a substantial extent, service enterprises have tended to follow their manufacturing clients abroad in order to preserve their market shares. Because of the inseparability of trade and foreign investment in service industries, the U.S. government has placed a high priority on the inclusion of the service sector in the forthcoming multilateral negotiations for the liberalization of World trade.

Base for Exports

In the case of establishment of a foreign affiliate as a base for exporting manufactures to the home market, to third-country markets, or both, cost factors dominate the decision to invest (whereas demand considerations are paramount in determining the locus of foreign investment for a local market). The principal attraction is the availability in the host country of a reliable and disciplined supply of low-cost labor. The parent company may then farm out its more labor-intensive products, processes, or components. This has been done in such industries as footwear, apparel, and consumer electronics.

An increasingly prominent share of foreign investment for export represents such vertical international specialization between different intermediate stages of production, in contrast with horizontal specialization between different final products. By locating different activities in various countries according to factor endowments, and by sourcing world-wide for components and other inputs, the transnational corporation has become an important vehicle through which developing countries can more fully realize their comparative advantage.

This process is a highly dynamic one. As the pace of development has accelerated in particular attractive locations, such as Singapore and Korea, the labor supply has tightened, and wages have been driven up. Investment for export based on cheap labor then moves on to other sites (e.g., Haiti and Sri Lanka) where an abundance of low-cost labor is still available.

In some cases, a foreign affiliate may become a base for exporting not because of any inherent cost advantage but because of performance requirements imposed by the host government. An investment undertaken originally to serve the local market may become subject to certain minimum export targets. Often, the requirement takes the form of mandating that a company offset its imports of materials and components with a comparable value of exports. As a result, foreign enterprises may be forced into uneconomic exporting while making up their losses through sales at high prices in the protected host-country market.[b]

[b]OECD, "Foreign Investment in Developing Countries," unpublished note by the Secretariat, 11 October 1984, p. 8.

Trends in Direct Investment

The flow of direct investment to the developing countries reached a peak of approximately $15 billion in 1981 (see Table 12). In the next two years it declined to only half that volume but picked up again in 1984. The 1981–1983 decline was partly a reflection of the world recession and austerity programs in the major host countries, which reduced profitability and therefore the volume of reinvested earnings.

Table 12

Net Flow of Direct Investment from Industrial Countries to Developing Countries, 1960 to 1983
(billions of U.S. dollars)

Year	Amount
1960-66 average	$1.8
1967-73 average	4.3
1974	1.1
1975	10.5
1976	7.9
1977	9.4
1978	10.8
1979	12.4
1980	10.5
1981	15.4
1982	10.4
1983	7.5
1984	10.0

Source: OECD as reproduced in IMF, Foreign Investment in Developing Counries, January 1985, p. 41. Figures for 1981-84 from OECD, Twenty Five Years of Development Cooperation, 1985 Report, Table 23, p. 331. These data differ somewhat from the direct investment figures in Table 7, which are based on national balance-of-payments statistics.

However, the recent fluctuations in investment should be viewed in relation to long-term trends.

In the early part of this century, foreign companies constructed railroads and electric power systems and developed mines and plantations. Later, investment in manufacturing and services became more important. Through the early 1970s, direct investment constituted between 20 and 25 percent of total capital flows from industrial to developing countries.[5]

Net flows of direct investment to the developing countries from all sources doubled in real terms between the early 1960s and the 1975–1982 period. However, its share in total capital flows declined because of the upsurge in bank lending during the latter period. Whereas direct investment constituted over half of all private capital flows to developing countries during the 1960s, it approximated only a quarter by the late 1970s. Nevertheless, net direct investment to non-oil-exporting developing countries grew by almost 3 percent a year in real terms during the 1970s.[6] A substantial share of the investment, amounting to more than half of the total, consisted of reinvested earnings rather than new flows of capital from the parent companies.

Recipients of Direct Investment

About three-quarters of total foreign direct investment has gone, not to the developing, but to the industrial countries. A rapidly increasing share has flowed to the United States. Between 1965 and 1969, only one-seventh of the flow of foreign direct investment to the industrial countries went to the United States; but by the 1980–1981 period, the U.S. share rose to one-half. Between the late 1970s and early 1980s, direct investment in all other developed areas declined not only as a proportion of the total but also in absolute terms (see Table 13).

The one-quarter of total direct investment that has flowed to the Third World has been highly concentrated in a few of the more advanced countries. Brazil and Mexico have been the major recipients, and Singapore has been the dominant destination in recent years in Asia. Together, these three countries account for almost half of the total flow to developing countries from all sources.[7]

For the less populous developing countries at the lower end of the income scale, direct investment has played only a minor role. Among the principal deterrents have been the small size of their domestic markets; the lack of skilled labor, natural resources, or a supportive infrastructure; the absence of an export-oriented manufacturing base; and political uncertainties in the host government's decision-making process.

The case of the People's Republic of China is particularly interesting because it shows that a strong public-sector role in industrialization is not necessarily a deterrent to foreign private investment. China has been receiving increasing amounts of direct investment: $200 million in 1979, $550 million in 1980, and more than $2 billion in 1981. The Foreign Investment Law of 1979 and subsequent regulations confirm the importance attached by China to the participation of foreign capital in its modernization.[8]

Sources of Direct Investment

The United States has been by far the principal source of direct investment in developing countries, accounting for almost 50 percent of

Table 13

Inward Direct Investment Flows, by Region and Selected Countries, 1965 to 1981
(millions of SDRs)

	CUMULATIVE VALUE OF FLOWS				SHARE OF FLOWS			
	1965-69	1970-74	1975-79	1980-81	1965-69	1970-74	1975-79	1980-81
All countries	32,590	58,006	105,085	76,527	100.0%	100.0%	100.0%	100.0%
Developed countries	25,546	50,400	75,761	55,899	78.4	86.9	72.1	73.0
United States	3,600	9,404	24,610	28,720	11.0	16.2	23.4	37.5
Europe	14,956	30,991	42,024	25,279	45.9	53.4	40.0	33.0
EC(6)[a]	9,001	20,929	22,788	13,147	27.6	36.1	21.7	17.2
United Kingdom	2,989	5,703	9,362	6,059	9.2	9.8	8.9	7.9
Other Europe	2,966	4,359	9,874	6,073	9.1	7.5	9.4	7.9
Canada	3,077	3,541	3,651	2,330	9.4	6.1	3.5	3.0
Japan	268	593	510	380	0.8	1.0	0.5	0.5
Other developed countries[b]	3,645	5,871	4,966	3,850	11.2	10.1	4.7	5.0

Developing countries	6,859	7,606	29,003	20,419	21.0	13.1	27.6	26.7
OPEC countries	1,793	-3,557	4,566	1,849	5.5	-6.1	4.3	2.4
Western Hemisphere[c]	3,520	6,712	14,715	10,783	10.8	11.6	14.0	14.1
Africa[c]	743	961	2,027	1,437	2.3	1.7	1.9	1.9
Asia and Middle East	802	3,490	7,696	6,350	2.5	6.0	7.3	8.3
Estimate for unreported flows	185	0	321	209	0.6	0.0	0.3	0.3

Note: All countries total includes IMF estimates for unreported flows, identified in this table as Estimate for unreported flows. Since these estimates are not allocated by country, developed and developing countries totals do not add to All countries. Otherwise, detail may not add to totals because of rounding.

[a] Includes Belgium, France, Germany, Italy, Luxembourg, and the Netherlands.
[b] Includes Australia, New Zealand, and South Africa.
[c] Excludes flows from OPEC countries which are shown separately.

Source: U.S. Department of Commerce, International Direct Investment, August 1984, p. 47. Based on: International Monetary Fund, Balance of Payments Statistics, 1982 Yearbook, Part 2, Vol. 33, Supplement to 1977 Yearbook, Vol. 27, and unpublished statistics for the years 1965-67, except for France, Germany, and the United Kingdom. Data for these countries for 1965-66 obtained from 1969, 1970, and 1972 Yearbooks.

the total. Other important sources have been the United Kingdom, Germany, Japan, and France. Between 1970 and 1982, however, the growth of investment from the three traditional suppliers (the United States, the United Kingdom, and France) has lagged substantially behind investment from Japan and Germany (see Table 14).

The major investing countries tend to concentrate their investments in particular areas, reflecting geographic propinquity, political and historical ties, and trade relations. More than 60 percent of U.S. direct investment in developing countries is in Latin America, whereas Asia is the principal recipient of Japanese investment. British investment goes mostly to Commonwealth countries, and French companies tend to focus on countries with past colonial ties in Africa and elsewhere.

A phenomenon of the past decade is the expanding volume of direct investment originating in the developing countries themselves. The total outflow of such investment from non-oil-exporting developing countries amounted to $640 million annually during 1980–1982, compared with $120 million a year during 1973–1975. Brazil, the Philippines, and Korea were the principal source countries.[9] In addition, a number of the major oil-exporting countries increased their foreign direct investments, mostly in the industrial countries.

Sectoral Composition

For each of the major source countries, manufacturing constitutes the main sector for investment. This is in marked contrast with the situation in the 1960s, when mining and petroleum were the major sectors for U.S. and Japanese investment in the Third World (see Table 15). For both countries, the share of mining and petroleum dropped from almost half of the total direct investment to approximately a quarter.

Foreign investment in public utilities was once substantial, especially in Latin America, but is now of minor importance. Utility companies were among the first to be nationalized; and in any case, their regulated prices depressed profitability and discouraged investment. The most rapidly growing sector for all major source countries other than the United Kingdom has been services, including trade, insurance, and finance.

Income Receipts

Recorded income receipts on direct investment from all developing countries rose from $10.4 billion in 1973 to a peak of $26.7 billion in 1981. Most of the increase came from the major oil-exporting countries, although income from non-oil-exporting developing countries also rose substantially. But income receipts fell to $17.7 billion in 1983 as a result of the world recession and the decline in oil prices.[10]

Table 14

Industrial Countries: Stock of Foreign Direct Investment in Developing Countries, 1970 and 1982
(billions of U.S. dollars)

	1970	1982	Avg. Annual Growth rate, 1970-82
Australia	0.3	1.5	14.4%
Belgium	0.8	2.1	8.4
Canada	1.7	4.5	8.5
France	3.8	9.6	8.0
Germany Fed. Rep. of	1.9	12.6	17.1
Italy	1.2	3.8	10.1
Japan	1.2	11.4†	20.6
Netherlands	2.2	5.3	7.6
Sweden	0.3	1.4	13.7
Switzerland	0.9	3.4	11.7
United Kingdom	5.9	15.8	8.6
United States	22.3	68.6	9.8
Other industrial countries††	0.2	1.1	15.3
Total	42.7	141.1	10.5

Note: This table uses end-of-year figures, and the OECD definition of developing countries, which differs from Fund classification. See Appendix I.

† Excludes official support for private investment (estimated at over $6 billion).

†† Austria, Denmark, Finland, New Zealand, and Norway

Source: International Monetary Fund, Foreign Investment in Developing Countries, p. 43. Based on: Organization of Economic Cooperation and Development, Investing in Developing Countries, 1983; Development Cooperation, 1983.

Table 15

Four Industrial Countries: Composition of Foreign Direct Investment Stock in Developing Countries, 1967 and 1980
(percent)

	1967[a]			1980[b]		
	Mining and Petroleum	Manufacturing	Other[c]	Mining and Petroleum	Manufacturing	Other[c]
United States	49.6	27.1	23.3	26.4	34.5	39.1
United Kingdom	12.5[d]	34.0	53.5	2.8[d]	54.4	42.8
Germany, Fed. Rep. of	7.5	85.0	7.5	3.9	72.4	23.7
Japan	44.4	33.6	22.0	24.0	42.7	33.3

[a] 1969 for Japan.
[b] 1978 for the United Kingdom.
[c] Mainly services, but also agriculture, public utilities, transport, and construction.
[d] Excludes investment in petroleum sector.

Source: International Monetary Fund, Foreign Investment in Developing Countries, p. 44. Based on: Organization for Economic Cooperation and Development, Stock of Private Direct Investments by DAC Countries in Developing Countries, End-1967; for U.S. data, U.S. Department of Commerce, Survey of Current Business, various issues; for U.K. data, Trade and Industry, Nov. 15, 1973, Business Monitor, May 1978 Supplement; for Japanese data, Ministry of International Trade and Industry and Economic Survey of Japan, 1980-81, Economic Planning Agency; for data on the Federal Republic of Germany, Monthly Report of the Deutsche Bundesbank, August 1982.

The burden of income payments by non-oil-exporting developing countries fell as a percentage of exports of goods and services over the 1973–1983 period. Whereas payments on direct investment amounted to 3 percent of exports in 1973, they declined gradually to less than 1.5 percent in 1983. In contrast, interest payments on external debt rose from 6 percent of exports of goods and services in 1973 to more than 13 percent in 1983.

A large proportion of earnings on direct investment is reinvested in the host country. For the non-oil-exporting developing countries that record information on this subject, an average of 52 percent of all direct investment earnings were reinvested during the 1973–1982 period. However, the proportion reinvested fluctuated substantially as changing conditions affected the profitability of new investment and hence the need to retain earnings to finance expanded operations.

In addition to profits on direct investment abroad, companies receive royalties and licensing fees in payment for the transfer of technology. Most, but not all, such payments are made between affiliates of the same parent company because direct investment is the main vehicle for the transfer of technology to developing countries. In 1982, for example, receipts of royalties and licensing fees from U.S. affiliates in developing countries amounted to $1.2 billion, equivalent to 85 percent of all such receipts from developing countries.

Although intrafirm receipts of royalties and licensing fees grew rapidly over the past decade, receipts from unrelated firms grew even more rapidly, especially from developing countries in Asia. This reflected the tendency toward *unbundling* (i.e., arrangements for the transfer of technology and management independent of direct investment capital).

Effects of Direct Investment

There is a presumption that foreign investment in developing countries is beneficial to both host and home governments. Otherwise, why would most developing countries have adopted special incentives to attract such investment and most industrial countries have special programs to encourage its outflow? However, the simple proposition of a mutuality of gain in the relationship is far from universally accepted. Despite a radical shift in the past decade toward greater receptivity in developing countries to foreign direct investment, suspicions linger on both sides.

Host Countries

The effects of foreign investment on host countries can be considered from two points of view: the external effects on the host's balance of payments and the internal effects on its economic growth.

External Effects. Foreign investment has occasionally been criticized in the United Nations and other North-South forums on the grounds that it takes more out of poor countries than it puts in. This criticism rests on a comparison of two annual flows: outflow of profits and interest from the developing countries to the multinationals and net inflows of capital from the multinationals to the host countries. Indeed, an excess of outflows of dividends and interest over inflows of capital has occurred for many years. For example, in 1980 and 1981, U.S. companies received incomes averaging more than $12 billion a year from direct investments in Third World countries while bringing in only about $6 billion on average in new capital.[11]

However, a juxtaposition of these two flows is meaningless. The flows bear no logical relationship to each other. The outflow of dividends and interest in a given year is related to the profitability of the cumulative investments of prior years, not to the inflow of capital in the same year. Moreover, as an indication of the balance-of-payments effects of direct investment on host countries, it is grossly misleading to look at only one item of receipts (capital inflows from parent companies) and to compare that with one item of payments (remittance of profits and interest).[12]

Instead, it is necessary to take into account the impact of foreign investment on all items in a country's balance-of-payments, particularly the volume of imports and exports. In the case of natural resource investment, for example, the bulk of the output is typically exported, contributing to the host country's foreign exchange receipts on the trade account. In manufacturing, even if the product is sold in the domestic market, it may substitute at least in part for imports, thereby resulting in a saving of foreign exchange. Sometimes, the effect may be indirect. For example, foreign investment in a fertilizer plant increases the availability of fertilizer to domestic agriculture, thus reducing the need for food imports.

A recent empirical study of the effect of U.S. foreign investment on host-country exports concluded that there was some evidence that U.S.-owned affiliates were leaders in expanding exports in most of the countries in which they operated. No indication was found that their presence inhibited the growth of host-country exports.[13]

Internal Effects. More fundamental than the balance-of-payments effects of foreign investment is the consequence for the host country's real income and economic growth. The essential case for foreign investment is that it brings in a package of resources that adds to the host country's real output and income an amount greater than that accruing to the investor. The difference must go to other groups: to labor in the form of more employment and higher wages; to consumers in the form of lower prices and a wider choice of better-quality products; and to the government in the form of larger tax revenues. As for government revenues, taxes on the profits of foreign enterprises constitute a large portion of the total tax receipts of a number of developing countries.

Given the benefits to the local economy from foreign investment, why has it been regarded with suspicion in much of the Third World, and why has so much controversy surrounded its operations? Historically, the explanation was the fear of domination of weak and often newly independent governments by powerful foreign companies controlling vital sectors of the domestic economy and in a position to exert political influence over local authorities. As Third World countries have grown stronger economically and matured politically, many of those more generalized fears have been dissipated. At the same time, certain other concerns remain that qualify an unequivocally favorable view.

Some of the most important effects are external to the company in that they are not reflected in market-determined costs of inputs and prices of outputs. These social costs and benefits take many forms. Among the oft-cited costs are the suppression of nascent local entrepreneurship by technologically superior foreign firms; the preemption of domestic capital by foreign firms that borrow locally and deprive indigenous firms of their main source of finance; and the monopolistic exploitation of market power through the control of patents and trademarks.

On the other hand, there are also social benefits, including the encouragement of domestic entrepreneurship by purchasing from or subcontracting to local suppliers; the training of workers in new skills and the spread of their knowledge to others in the labor force; and the stimulus to production in other sectors where a scarcity of inputs may be relieved by the products of the foreign enterprise.

Evaluation of the contribution of foreign enterprise is made difficult not only by considerations of external costs and benefits but also because a company's internal accounting may be distorted by host-government policies. The true value of a firm's output sold in the domestic market may be exaggerated by high prices resulting from protection against imports of comparable finished products. Equipment, components, and materials may be imported at artificially low prices because of an overvalued exchange rate maintained through a system of exchange controls.[14]

At the root of much of the controversy about the effects of direct investment on host countries is the confusion arising from mistaken attribution. If a country's overvalued exchange rate induces a firm to import more machinery and employ less labor than it otherwise would, is the firm to be blamed, or is the problem one of government policy? If protection of the domestic market induces uneconomic investment that is costly to the local economy, where does the responsibility for this distortion lie? And is the distortion any greater because the investor is a foreign enterprise rather than a domestic firm? Unquestionably, there are problems that are peculiar to the operations of foreign affiliates such as the opportunities to manipulate transfer prices on intrafirm transactions. But many of the alleged costs associated with foreign investment are actually reflections of inappropriate host-government policies and have little to do with the fact that the enterprise is an affiliate of a foreign company.

Although the costs and benefits of specific direct investments depend on the circumstances of each country and each project, it is generally acknowledged that the relationship can be one of mutual gain for both host country and foreign investor. Moreover, the attractiveness of a country to potential investors and the net benefits to host countries can be strongly affected by the host governments' economic policies.

Home Countries

Fears have been expressed in the United States that foreign direct investment leads to the loss of production, jobs, and exports for the domestic economy. This concern applies especially to manufacturing. In the primary and service sectors, investment abroad generally occurs because the alternative competitive opportunities at home are few or nonexistent. Minerals are produced where the ore bodies and fuel reserves are located. In the case of the service sector, selling to a foreign market is often possible only by setting up operations locally because of technological conditions or regulatory restrictions. Moreover, the export of services back to the home country is rare, so that the direct displacement effect in terms of jobs or exports tends to be small.

The critical issue in manufacturing is the assumption of what would happen if the investment does not take place. Much of U.S. investment in manufacturing abroad is intended to serve the host-country market. Most often, it is induced by trade restrictions; but in some cases, the motivation may be to avoid high transport costs or to achieve more efficient integration of production, marketing, and after-sale servicing. Generally, the alternative of manufacturing at home and exporting to the developing country does not exist. If American firms had not invested abroad, the chances are that firms based in other industrial countries would have. Thus, the displacement of U.S. jobs or exports does not normally occur. On the other hand, U.S.-owned foreign manufacturing subsidiaries catering to a host-country market support U.S. jobs to the extent that they are substantial purchasers of parent-company parts and components and U.S. capital goods.[15]

Similar reasoning applies to direct investment in developing countries primarily for export back to the United States or to third countries. To the extent that such investment occurs because of a fundamental shift in cost advantages to Third World countries (e.g., low-priced shoes), the continuation of production in the United States on the same scale as before would not be viable. Worker displacement from particular jobs does occur, and programs should be instituted to facilitate adjustment to other jobs more in keeping with U.S. comparative advantage.[16] The alternative of protecting our noncompetitive sectors would be a costly and inefficient way of dealing with the problem.

Over the long run, U.S. workers stand to gain both directly and indirectly from U.S. investment abroad in response to lower-cost foreign opportunities. Jobs are upgraded as workers move from older, less competitive industries to new, more sophisticated ones. In addition, labor gains from favorable feedbacks to the U.S. economy: U.S. investments abroad increase foreign incomes, some of which is spent on imports from the United States; and remitted earnings are available for new investment in the more advanced sectors of the American economy, where wages are higher.

On the other hand, when the foreign competitive advantage is due to an overvalued dollar or to subsidies paid by foreign governments, the relocation of American manufacturing facilities abroad represents a distortion in the allocation of resources. However rational the move may be from the perspective of the individual company, it is uneconomic and disruptive from the standpoint of society as a whole, and it imposes costly adjustments, particularly on American labor. The remedy lies not in treating the symptoms of the problem by restricting the outflow of U.S. investment but in vigorously addressing the underlying causes.

Host-Country Policies

All countries have the sovereign right to determine the conditions under which both domestic and foreign enterprises operate within their borders. At the same time, it must be recognized that multinational firms cannot be forced to locate in a particular country; they can only be attracted.[17]

Most developing countries have special programs of incentives and concessions to attract foreign enterprise, sometimes at substantial cost to the local economy. But the most important factors affecting the decision to invest are the relative stability of the political, social, and economic conditions and the prospect of earning a profit without having to rely on special government favors.

Host-government policies affecting foreign investment are of two broad types: general economic policies applicable to the economy as a whole and policies specifically directed to, or having a strong impact on, foreign investment.

General Economic Policies

The most important general policies fall into the macroeconomic category: fiscal, monetary, and exchange rate policies. Investors seek a reasonable degree of stability in the macroeconomic environment. Expanding budgetary deficits accommodated by easy money and leading to spiraling inflation and a depreciating currency are hardly conducive to investing for the long term. Economic instability may not be an absolute deterrent (e.g., Chile and Argentina in the 1950s and 1960s), but it nevertheless does discourage both domestic and foreign investment.

An inflationary host-country environment is especially discouraging to the foreign investor because of two special risks to which the investor is exposed. One is the exchange risk: A rapidly depreciating host-country currency means a compression of earnings when converted into the home-country currency. The other is the inconvertibility risk: A serious deterioration of the balance-of-payments and depletion of host-country reserves may lead to the restriction or suspension of the right to remit profits. Even though industrial countries generally offer insurance against inconvertibility, a foreign firm is unlikely to initiate a new investment at a time when the suspension of remittances is imminent or already in effect.

On the microeconomic side, some of the Southeast Asian countries have pointed the way to policies that increase the flow and enhance the contribution of direct investment. These are the policies of an open development strategy where market prices for both factors and products reflect resource scarcities. When this approach has been adopted, real interest rates have been positive, and prices of local resources generally have been allowed to conform to opportunity costs. Because trade restrictions are low, the bias of production in favor of the domestic as opposed to the export market is reduced, and investment is geared more closely to the country's comparative advanage.

Noninflationary macroeconomic policies and reliance on market pricing for goods and factors are the key to providing the right signals for investors, whether domestic or foreign. At the same time, they provide an environment of stability necessary to induce foreign enterprises to consider investment opportunities. By and large, foreign investors would rather cope with the vicissitudes of the market than contend with the arbitrariness of government decisionmaking, especially when the governments are not their own.

Policies Toward Foreign Investment

Host-government policies toward foreign investment are of five types: official screening and approval policies; investment incentives; performance requirements; restrictions on the repatriation of income; and policies relating to nationalization and dispute settlement.

Official Screening. Many developing countries exclude foreign investors from certain sectors. In some cases, this is justified on the grounds of political sensitivity (e.g., banking, broadcasting, publishing); in others, because the reserved sectors are deemed to be the commanding heights of the economy (e.g., public utilities, petroleum, steel). At the other extreme, some activities with relatively simple technical and financial requirements (e.g., retail and wholesale trade) are reserved for the local population. The takeover of existing local enterprises is also commonly prohibited.

In addition to the outright exclusion of foreign investment from certain sectors, some countries limit the extent of foreign ownership. Nigeria, for example, allows foreign participation in designated industries in accordance with the industry's technological complexity and capital requirements. Other countries (e.g., India, Mexico, the Philippines) generally limit foreign investors to a minority equity position, although most will permit majority or even 100 percent foreign ownership in some high-priority sectors or where production is mainly for export.[18] Mandatory divestment rules are a major element of foreign investment policy in some countries (e.g, India and Nigeria). Under this policy, foreign companies are required to release ownership and management control gradually by selling shares to residents over a specified period of time. The common regime for foreign investment of the Andean Pact countries incorporates such dilution requirements.

Restrictions on the share of foreign ownership may create substantial disincentives to foreign investment, especially in high-technology industries, where firms are concerned about protecting proprietary information. There is also a risk to the local economy in attempting to unduly accelerate the indigenization of foreign companies before domestic enterprise is in a position to take their place. And the outright exclusion of foreign investment from particular sectors may give domestic enterprise a monopoly position that inhibits development. For all these reasons, we believe that discriminatory restrictions against foreign enterprise do not serve the interests of developing countries.

Recognizing, however, that some host governments will continue to limit the scope of foreign enterprise, such restrictions should be applied on a most-favored-nation basis (i.e., equal treatment for foreign firms regardless of their nationality). Moreover, the administrative procedures for screening can themselves be a major deterrent to foreign investment. We therefore recommend greater clarity in the rules and streamlined administrative procedures for clearances and licenses. In those sectors where foreign enterprises do have the right of establishment, the host-country policy should be national treatment (i.e., treatment under national laws, regulations, and administrative practices that is no less favorable than that accorded to domestic enterprises, subject to mutually agreed-upon exceptions). National treatment, however, is far from an ironclad guarantee of nondiscrimination. Certain types of regulations, such as performance requirements and limitations on remittance abroad of profits, may nominally apply to domestic as well as foreign firms, but their impact is overwhelmingly discriminatory in practice. Such discriminatory regulations and practices should be eliminated.

Investment Incentives. A serious problem with incentives to attract foreign capital arises from differences in laws and practices in host and home countries. In the tax area, for example, many developing countries are reluctant to grant concessions because their effect is offset in the foreign investor's country. It is essential to improve communication between host and home countries so that differences in laws and practices are better understood and conflicts minimized.

Incentives to attract foreign capital take a wide variety of forms. Most fall into one of two categories: factor incentives affecting the cost or profitability of capital and labor used in production and commodity incentives affecting the prices of goods bought or sold by a firm.

Factor incentives include concessions such as tax holidays, accelerated depreciation, investment credits, loans at below-market interest rates, wage subsidies, and training grants. Far more important than special incentives, however, are the fundamentals affecting the profitability of an operation: the size and growth of the host-country market, the quality of the local labor force, the stability of the regulatory and administrative environment, and the soundness of the host government's general economic policies. If these conditions are unsatisfactory, special incentives are unlikely to be effective. However, if the fundamentals are satisfactory, special incentives may influence the choice of country location at the margin.

Intense competition among developing countries in granting financial inducements can be a quite costly negative-sum game. If an agreement to limit special incentives could be negotiated, it would be in the long-run interest of all developing countries.

Among the main types of commodity incentives that alter the prices of goods bought or sold are tariffs and quotas on competing imports and exemptions from import duties or other restrictions on inputs. Such inducements are especially important for investments aimed at the host-country market.

Protection, regardless of the form it takes, is a subsidy to domestic producers. In this case, the subsidy is financed, not by payments from the government treasury, but by direct payments from consumers to producers in the form of higher prices than those that would prevail without the protection.

Multinational companies are sometimes criticized for being in the best position to take advantage of this implicit subsidy by locating their affiliates behind the shelter of the protective barriers. According to this view, the resulting stimulus to industrialization may provide little benefit to domestic enterprise while imposing costs on the local economy in the form of higher prices to consumers and possibly excessive profits to the foreign affiliates insulated from international competition.

To the extent that there is a problem here, it is essentially one of misguided foreign trade policies on the part of the developing country rather than exploitative behavior on the part of the multinational firm. Given the opportunity, most foreign manufacturing firms seeking to sell in a Third World market would prefer to export from a home base rather than produce locally. The main exceptions are companies producing bulk products, such as paper goods or building materials, for which high transport costs make shipment from the home country impractical. Companies in these fields generally neither need nor seek protection.

Infant industry protection is a widespread phenomenon in the Third World. It will best advance the host country's interest if it is a rationally designed policy in which the costs of protection are carefully weighed against the gains from stimulating industrialization. The trouble with most protection is that it is indiscriminate in the industries favored, excessive in the degree of shelter granted, too long-lasting, and most important, overly reliant on direct controls. Unlike tariffs, direct controls, such as import quotas, break the link between domestic and international prices and prevent the market from performing its function as allocator of resources.

Apart from this disadvantage, reliance on direct controls produces adverse side effects on the investment climate. If an import quota is imposed, someone decides who gets the licenses to import. The substitution of administrative decision for the market as an allocator of scarce imports can place an enormous strain on precisely those types of administrative skills that are often in short supply in developing countries. Moreover, the temptation to corruption is great when low-income civil servants must make decisions about the allocation of import licenses that may have great value to the recipients.

One of the most important causes of bureaucratic delays, arbitrary decisions, and widespread corruption in developing countries is excessive reliance on direct controls. We therefore recommend that when governments intervene to promote legitimate social and economic objectives, they do so insofar as possible through measures that work through the market and are reflected in price signals rather than through direct controls.

Performance Requirements. An increasing number of countries impose obligations on foreign firms in the form of minimum export levels or local-content requirements.

The effects of minimum export requirements are similar to those of export subsidies in that they artificially increase the level of exports. Such exports may displace another country's home production or its sales to third markets. Losses by the foreign enterprise in mandated uneconomic exports can usually be offset by exploiting protected positions in the host-country market.

Local-content requirements artificially reduce imports by mandating that a minimum percentage of the value of the final product be produced locally or purchased from local sources. These value-added requirements are similar to import quotas. Often, the two types of obligations are combined by linking a firm's permitted imports to the value of its exports so that no net foreign exchange cost is entailed by its operations.

Performance requirements pressure firms to engage in economic behavior inconsistent with market forces. They distort trade and investment flows, lead to uneconomic use of resources, and harm the interests of other countries. We believe performance requirements should be strongly discouraged by the World Bank and the IMF in the context of the economic advice they give to developing countries. Moreover, an effort should be made in the forthcoming round of GATT trade negotiations to develop new provisions that would constrain the use of these distortive devices by developed and developing countries alike.

Serious concern about performance requirements has been expressed by American labor and industry.[19] Congress responded to such concerns by including in the Tariff and Trade Act of 1984 a provision directing the U.S. Trade Representative to enter into consultations with any country imposing export performance requirements adversely affecting U.S. interests and authorizing the representative to restrict imports of products subject to such requirements.[20] We recommend that this explicit authority be employed to discourage the use of performance requirements pending the adoption of internationally agreed-upon rules in a new round of trade negotiations.

Restrictions on Repatriation of Income. In many developing countries, restrictions are placed on the remittance of income on direct investment in the form of interest and dividends as well as royalties and fees on the transfer of technology.

In some countries, the restrictions are part of their permanent direct investment policies. The amounts allowed to be repatriated may be limited to a proportion of the firm's foreign exchange earnings or may be subject to additional taxation. In Brazil, for example, when the average remittance over a three-year period exceeds 12 percent of the registered capital including reinvested earnings, supplementary taxes are imposed: 40 percent of the remittances between 12 and 15 percent; 50 percent of remittances between 15 and 25 percent; and 60 percent of remittances above 25 percent of invested capital.[21]

In other countries, income can be transferred abroad without special limitations except for temporary restrictions applied as part of broader exchange controls during periods of serious external imbalance. Such emergency measures have proliferated as a result of the debt-repayment problems of many developing countries and, in some countries, have been superimposed on the permanent restrictions.

There is little doubt that limitations on the remittance of income are major deterrents to new investment. Early lifting at least of the emergency restrictions and some assurance to foreign investors that they will not be reimposed in the future may prove necessary to encourage a significant recovery of foreign investment.

Limitations on remittances have other unfortunate effects. They are likely to encourage disguised remittances through artificial transfer prices in transactions between affiliates of a multinational firm. The result is a reduction in the host country's share of taxes on profits. In addition, where dividends are subject to greater restrictions than interest payments on loans, encouragement is given to excessive proportions of debt to equity in the foreign enterprise's capital structure.

Nationalization and Dispute Settlement. The threat of nationalization is a major deterrent to new foreign investment and also discourages the continued operation of existing foreign enterprises. In the event of expropriation of the property of multinational enterprises, the action not only should be subject to due process under the laws of the host country but also should be nondiscriminatory and conform to the internationally accepted standard of prompt, adequate, and effective compensation. Inclusion of these principles in the laws of host countries and in treaties between host and home governments would contribute significantly to improving the investment climate.

Formal provisions cannot, however, fully protect a company against arbitrary and inequitable actions. A determined government can achieve de facto nationalization without outright expropriation through measures such as unreasonable price controls, profit limitations, or confiscatory taxes. The result is *creeping expropriation.*

Even with the best intentions, it is difficult to determine equitable compensation in the case of nationalization. Simple definitions such as net book value fail to compensate a company for lost profit opportunities or investments in intangible assets such as goodwill or the development of marketing channels. Formulas based on the capitalization of earning capacity also have limitations. The best way to resolve disputes over compensation for nationalized property would be to incorporate in the original investment agreement a provision for recourse, at the request of either party, to international arbitration or other specified dispute-settlement facilities.

U.S. Policies

In September 1983, the White House released a major policy statement on international investment. Its underlying principle is that "foreign investment flows which respond to private market forces will lead to more efficient international production and thereby benefit both home and host countries."[22] The statement calls attention to the widespread and distortive intervention by governments and the lack of a system of international rules and institutions for international investment comparable to GATT and the IMF in the fields of international trade and finance. It also expresses the determination of the U.S. government to pursue bilateral and multilateral efforts to achieve a more open global climate for international investment. We applaud this more activist U.S. government policy.

Trade and Investment

Trade and investment flows have always been closely linked. An open world trading system is one of the most important conditions for ensuring that investment flows correspond to the pull of market forces. Just as import substitution policies have artificially induced foreign investment in developing countries behind the shelter of protective walls, import restrictions in the United States distort the flow of investment. Restrictions on clothing imports, for example, have undoubtedly discouraged U.S. investment in clothing industries in developing countries. Because efficient world investment is inseparable from an open world trading system, we strongly endorse the leadership taken by the U.S. government in launching a new round of multilateral negotiations to liberalize world trade and to improve and strengthen the rules under which it is carried out.

Taxation

The two long-standing pillars of U.S. law on the taxation of foreign investment are the deferral and credit provisions of the Internal Revenue Code. Corporate income taxes on the earnings of subsidiaries are deferred until the profits are remitted to the parent company. In addition, a credit is given against a parent company's U.S. tax liability for income taxes paid by its affiliates to host countries.

Insurance

The principal specific U.S. inducement for private investment in developing countries is the insurance and financing facilities of the Overseas Private Investment Corporation (OPIC). For a fee, OPIC insures new investments against the risk of loss due to currency inconvertibility, expropriation (including creeping expropriation), and war, revolution, insurrection, or civil strife. In addition, OPIC provides small amounts of direct financing and credit guarantees to private U.S. financial institutions that extend loans to eligible U.S. investors in Third World projects.[23] Special consideration is given to projects in the poorest countries and to those sponsored by smaller American firms.

Since 1981 OPIC has issued record annual volumes of insurance, increasing from $1.5 billion in fiscal 1981 to $4.2 billion in fiscal 1984. Because a firm may take out more than one policy to cover different types of risks, the actual increase in insured U.S. investments was less. Nevertheless, the total amount of U.S. investment in OPIC-insured projects increased from $0.9 billion in fiscal 1980 to $1.6 billion in fiscal 1984. We believe that even more use would be made of OPIC insurance if its presently sluggish decisionmaking process were accelerated.

Are the investments insured by OPIC additional to what would have occurred anyway in the absence of the insurance? According to a study done for the agency, 25 percent of the investments covered by OPIC would not have taken place without a guarantee; 18 percent would have occurred anyway; and in the remaining 57 percent, although the evidence was not conclusive, the guarantee did appear essential in many cases.[24]

OPIC is self-sustaining, having earned more than $97 million in fiscal 1984. Although it has ample authority for its political risk insurance program, it has requested additional authority but no new appropriations for direct loans and commercial guarantees. We recommend a substantial expansion of OPIC's very limited present authority to make loans and to issue commercial guarantees for direct investments in developing countries. This can be accomplished by removing the limit in the authorizing legislation on the amount of OPIC's earned income that may be allocated to these purposes after the provision of reserves.

Because of the concern of U.S. farm, labor, and industry groups about developing country competition in the U.S. market, certain types of projects are excluded from OPIC support by policy or statute. Among the exclusions are the production or processing of competitive agricultural products such as palm oil and sugar, and so-called runaway plants to produce manufactured products for export back to the United States.

We appreciate the reasons for excluding OPIC support for projects to produce products for export back to the United States in competition with domestic production. However, such Third World products should not also be subject to special import restrictions in the U.S. market when they are produced abroad without benefit of government subsidies or other artificial incentives.

Bilateral Investment Treaties

In late 1981, the United States launched a program to negotiate bilateral investment treaties. This program is a major instrument for advancing the Reagan Administration's objective of encouraging market-directed private foreign investment to play a stepped-up role in the world economy.[25]

The objective of the program is to improve the investment climate in recipient countries by providing a stable and predictable legal framework that includes certain protections and guarantees to foreign investors. Under the bilateral investment treaty prototype agreement, both parties agree to extend national and most-favored-nation treatment to new and established investments, subject to exceptions declared by each party in the agreement; to provide for unrestricted transfers of profits, dividends, capital, and compensation; to conform to requirements of international law regarding the expropriation of a foreign investor's property, including prompt, adequate, and effective compensation; and to follow certain procedures for the settlement of investment disputes, including, when requested by an investor, recourse to binding third-party arbitration. In addition, the treaties include certain nonbinding, hortatory provisions such as "each party will endeavor to avoid imposing" trade-related performance requirements on the investments of the other party.

In 1986, the Administration submitted ten bilateral investment treaties to the Senate for advice and consent to ratification. These treaties, the first signed under the program, are with Bangladesh, Cameroon, Egypt, Grenada, Haiti, Morocco, Panama, Senegal, Turkey, and Zaire. Six treaty partners have already ratified the agreements. A dozen treaties are now under negotiation with countries such as Malaysia, the People's Republic of China, El Salvador, Uruguay, and Costa Rica.

The treaties promise benefits to both investors and host countries. For the investor, they provide the prospect of stability and predictability with respect to the most sensitive areas of host government policy; for the host country, they offer the prospect of enlarged flows of foreign investment. Even where the effort to negotiate treaties is unsuccessful, the dialogue surrounding the negotiations can be an effective means of educating developing country officials about the benefits of foreign investment and the conditions necessary to attract it.

Thus far, no developing country with substantial U.S. private investment has signed or initialed a bilateral investment treaty. By and large, those that have accepted the provisions are relatively small countries or countries with little appeal to investors. Among the obstacles to wider acceptance of the treaties are the provisions for unrestricted transfer of earnings and capital and the right of the investor to binding third-party arbitration in the case of disputes.

An important issue is whether the United States should be willing to negotiate more limited understandings with countries not yet prepared to negotiate a full-scale treaty.[26] For example, most bilateral treaties negotiated with developing countries by European countries allow restrictions on transfers in case of exceptional balance-of-payments stringency. As for dispute settlement, many Latin American countries adhere to the so-called Calvo doctrine requiring investors to seek remedies entirely within the local law and juridical system of the host country. Adherence to this doctrine rules out acceptance of the binding third-party arbitration provision of the U.S. prototype treaty.[27]

In recognition of the diverse circumstances of individual developing countries, we believe that the United States should be prepared to negotiate agreements containing more limited commitments than those included in a complete bilateral investment treaty. By being flexible on some subjects, such as transfers and binding arbitration, it should be possible to gain the important remaining benefits of the treaty. The more limited agreements or understandings could be negotiated for defined periods. They should be viewed, not as inferior substitutes, but as stepping-stones toward full bilateral investment treaties.

International Policies

Various efforts have been made at the international level in recent years to facilitate or establish norms for the operations of transnational corporations. The most important current international initiatives relate to codes of conduct, investment insurance, and the protection of intellectual property rights.

Codes of Conduct

An appealing idea over the years has been a general agreement or code of conduct for international investment comparable to GATT for international trade and the IMF Articles of Agreement for international finance.[28] Actually, the industrial countries reached agreement on a set of voluntary guidelines in 1976 under the auspices of the OECD. The guidelines set down standards for the behavior of transnational companies and for their treatment by host and home countries. However, they apply only among the industrial countries.

About the same time that the OECD guidelines were adopted, the United Nations launched its project to negotiate a worldwide code to which both developed and developing countries could subscribe. Although addressing essentially the same range of subjects, the UN effort includes much more detail and reflects a more ambitious effort at standard setting. But after almost ten years of negotiation, the developed and developing countries are still far apart on important issues, and the ultimate prospects for the code are uncertain.

The main responsibility for policy regarding transnational enterprises must continue to reside with national governments and to be reflected in national laws, regulations, and practices.[29] Nevertheless, a constructive role can be played by the negotiation of general international guidelines. The negotiations themselves serve an educational purpose by highlighting points of consensus as well as areas that require further efforts at conflict resolution. Moreover, the standards incorporated in the code can provide points of departure for national policy and legislation tailored to the situation of individual host countries.

We believe that the basic principles underlying the OECD guidelines should be included in any universal code relating to transnational enterprises. Specifically, we endorse the following elements: voluntary standards rather than legally binding commitments; recognition of responsibilities of both governments and transnationals; the application of guidelines to all international investors, whether private, state-owned, or mixed companies; and inclusion of the principles of respect for international law and national treatment once a foreign enterprise is established.

Investment Insurance

The idea of an international agency to insure foreign investors against noncommercial risks has been around since the late 1950s. Under the leadership of former President A. W. Clausen of the World Bank, the idea was revived and developed into a full-blown draft convention for the establishment of MIGA. The draft has been approved by the board of governors of the Bank and awaits the requisite ratifications by governments.

The purpose of MIGA would be to improve the prospects for foreign private investment in developing countries by issuing insurance against the so-called transfer, breach of government contract, and war risks (the latter including civil unrest and public violence) and by supplementing the activities of the World Bank and the IFC in promoting foreign investment through research, information, and technical assistance and more generally by encouraging host countries to adopt policies conducive to direct investment.

Because all DAC countries operate their own national investment-guarantee programs,[30] a natural question is what additional insurance functions would be performed by a new international agency. According to the general counsel of the World Bank, MIGA would complement rather than compete with national programs by operations such as: guaranteeing investments in countries where the national agency is already heavily exposed or in countries that do not have a national program; guaranteeing types of investments (e.g., service contracts) or risks (e.g., breach of host-government undertakings) not covered under national programs; coguaranteeing large investments and thus avoiding excessive risk concentration; and providing reinsurance of national guarantee agencies as another means of risk diversification. Some think that MIGA's authority should be flexible enough to include the guarantee of the present value of existing developing country debt as a way of helping to resolve the international debt crisis.

As currently conceived, MIGA would be an autonomous and self-supporting agency with some ties to the World Bank. It would be financed jointly by home and host countries, with voting power divided equally between them as groups when all eligible countries join. However, certain important decisions would be made on the basis of special majorities reflecting the financial contributions of members.

Only investments specifically approved by the host country would be underwritten by the agency. In determining the eligibility of projects for insurance, MIGA should exercise care to ensure that the same high standards are applied as those used by the IFC.

We believe MIGA's most important contribution may well lie not so much in its additional insurance facilities but in the confidence-building framework it could provide for host and home countries and private investors. In order to reinforce the credibility of MIGA in the eyes of investors and host countries, a close link should be established between MIGA and the World Bank.[31]

Intellectual Property

The protection of intellectual property rights is becoming increasingly important for the flow of direct investment into both developed and developing countries. The inadequacy of protection in many countries today is a major disincentive to investment in manufacturing facilities and to the transfer of technology. Moreover, U.S. competitiveness at home and abroad depends increasingly on U.S. research and development capability and the technology it generates. Yet this country's ability to recover costs worldwide has eroded not only through price controls and restricted market access but often because of competition from local producers who pirate U.S. products, processors, and know-how.

Pirating also harms the countries that engage in it because it discourages indigenous research. In the case of developing countries, it exacerbates their technological dependence on the industrial countries, a condition about which they have long expressed serious concern.

The U.S. government should urge countries as a matter of priority to enact effective legislation for the protection of patents and trademarks and to adhere to the Paris Industrial Property Convention. In the current negotiations for the revision of the Paris Convention, the United States should resist efforts to weaken its provisions.

At present, this country has little power to influence the international copyright system. There are two major international treaties dealing with copyright: the Berne Convention for the Protection of Literary and Artistic Works and the Universal Copyright Code (UCC). The United States is not a member of the Berne Convention,[32] nor is it any longer a part of the UCC power structure, given its recent withdrawal from the United Nations Educational, Scientific, and Cultural Organization (UNESCO), which administers the treaty.

U.S. adherence to the Berne Convention, which provides greater copyright protection than the UCC, would increase its ability to pursue more stringent international copyright regulations and to urge other countries to abide by them. The United States would also be able to influence the work of the World Intellectual Property Organization (WIPO), which administers the Berne treaty and is considered the predominant copyright organization.[33]

We support the Administration's plan, announced in April 1986,[34] to move toward adherence to the Berne treaty while including protection for intellectual property rights as a major negotiating objective in current and prospective trade and investment negotiations. WIPO will be an invaluable source of aid in the latter regard because GATT is not a technical organization and would need WIPO copyright expertise.[35] Gaining WIPO's support in this endeavor will be less difficult if the United States is a member of the Berne Convention.

Portfolio Equity Investment

Portfolio equity investment in the Third World is a small but increasing source of capital for development. In contrast with debt financing, the host country bears no servicing burden if the investment falters. And in contrast with direct investment, the host country does not have the problems, real or perceived, associated with foreign control of domestic industry because the equity investor seeks only a share of the profits, not the responsibilities of control.

International Investors

For the foreign investor, equity investment in the developing countries offers substantial benefits, including the possibility of high returns. In recent years, the total annual return in U.S. dollars in emerging Third World markets has been substantially higher than that of the world's major equity markets: 20 percent compared with 12 percent (see Table 16). Moreover, equity investment provides an especially attractive vehicle for risk diversification for the investor because of the lack of synchronization between returns in industrialized and developing countries.

Pension funds are the largest institutional purchasers of equities. In the United States there are no restrictions on the amount of private pension fund assets that may be invested abroad. However, most state and local pension funds are legally prohibited from investing in foreign securities.

In recent years private pension funds have substantially increased their holdings of foreign equities. From 1977 to 1980 the proportion of pension funds of the *Fortune* top 100 industrials holding foreign equities had doubled to 34 percent and had increased from 7 to 29 percent among the next 100. For U.S. pension funds in general, foreign commitments totaled $16 billion at the end of 1984, double the amount two years earlier.

The situation is similar in Britain and Japan. At the end of 1982, 15 percent of the assets of British pension funds were invested in foreign equities, a ratio more than double that of three years earlier. In Japan, foreign equity investment was prohibited until 1979. The rate of growth has been rapid since then, and Japanese pension funds now hold more than 8 percent of their assets in foreign securities.[36]

The growth in foreign equity investment has been due not only to the recognition of its benefits but also to a relaxation of restrictions by industrial countries. In 1974, the United States abolished the interest equalization tax, which affected most purchases of foreign securities. In that same year, the Employee Retirement and Income Security Act (ERISA)

Table 16

Return on Investment in Emerging Markets, 1976 to 1983
(percent)

Country Group	1976	1977	1978	1979	1980	1981	1982	1983	Avg. annual return 1976–83
Emerging markets									
Argentina	134.8	-44.7	80.3	232.3	-17.2	-52.7	-66.4	54.7	5.9
Brazil	4.0	9.3	-1.1	-12.5	4.1	-9.0	-14.7	31.6	0.5
Chile	92.2	146.3	56.3	131.6	92.7	-48.3	-52.1	-20.0	27.7
Hong Kong	40.0	-11.0	18.0	80.0	71.0	-16.0	-42.0	-8.6	9.2
India	34.1	13.7	51.2	21.1	42.3	23.8	-5.9	8.2	22.0
Jordan[a]	-	-	51.7	28.0	21.1	35.0	8.0	-6.5	19.9
Korea	72.4	114.2	23.7	-13.0	-26.5	50.0	8.8	-4.9	20.8
Mexico	-19.1	22.3	127.8	96.3	17.7	-34.5	-78.7	136.1	6.9
Singapore	14.0	6.0	52.0	-12.0	29.0	15.0	-1.0	29.2	15.0
Thailand	0.4	187.7	43.2	-40.7	-12.9	-19.2	-18.7	9.7	12.3
Zimbabwe	-11.6	-5.7	-14.4	179.3	50.3	-56.7	-32.4	-24.1	-4.9

Industrial countries									
United States	23.0	-8.0	6.0	14.0	29.0	-14.0	21.0	20.0	13.5
Japan	25.0	15.0	52.0	-12.0	29.0	15.0	-1.0	23.0	16.8
Cumulative return									
Capital International World Index[b]	114.0	116.0	136.0	152.0	192.0	184.0	205.0	250.0	12.1
IFC emerging market index[c]	131.0	184.0	276.0	432.0	531.0	467.0	341.0	434.0	20.1

Note: The returns depicted are calculated as follows: Assume a U.S. investor has $100 to invest in an emerging market. After conversion to domestic currency, the proceeds are placed in a basket of actively traded stocks. Dividends may be paid on the investment during the year, and capital gains may also be secured if the market price of the stock rises. These two sources of income are converted back to U.S. dollars at year-end exchange rates to yield a return denominated in U.S. dollars. This return is expressed as a percentage of the original $100 investment.

[a] Jordan's stock market opened in January 1978, hence data are not available for earlier years.
[b] Based on Capital International data; January 1, 1976 = 100.
[c] Returns in emerging markets included in this table; except for Hong Kong and Singapore, on a market-weighted basis (1980 for 1975-80, individual years for 1981-83), January 1, 1976 = 100.

Source: World Bank, *World Development Report 1985*, p. 135, as subsequently revised by World Bank staff.

was enacted. One aspect of its regulation of U.S. pension funds is the encouragement of risk diversification and therefore foreign equity investment. During the 1970s, Japan liberalized restrictions on the outflow of capital, and Britain abolished exchange controls.

Foreign equity investment remains overwhelmingly in the securities of the OECD countries. British pension funds have the bulk of their foreign equity investments in Japanese and U.S. securities. The only developing countries in which they have any sizable investment are in the Pacific basin, notably, Hong Kong, Korea, and Singapore. Approximately 90 percent of all U.S. pension fund foreign equity investment is in OECD countries. Of the remaining 10 percent, 90 percent flows to only three countries: Hong Kong, Singapore, and South Africa. The only other developing countries to benefit significantly from the equity investments of U.S. pension funds are Israel and Malaysia.

Life insurance companies also have huge sums for investment, but they have a much smaller percentage in foreign equities than the pension funds. A major reason is the heavy regulation of U.S. life insurance companies by state authorities, which typically restrict the proportion of assets that can be invested abroad. Generally, U.S. companies may invest only up to 6 percent of their assets in all foreign countries other than Canada.

In Japan, life insurance companies are restricted to investing no more than 10 percent of their assets in foreign securities. Although there are no quantitative limits on foreign equity investment for British life insurance companies, they are nonetheless restricted. Companies may hold only securities that are quoted on a stock exchange approved by the Department of Trade. The only developing countries that have approved stock exchanges are Hong Kong, Singapore, Malaysia, Brazil, and Mexico.

Constraints by industrial country governments on the outflow of capital should be removed. Specifically, restrictions on the proportion of an insurance company's portfolio that can be placed in foreign equities should be abolished. Public pension funds should be permitted to invest in foreign equities.

Host Countries

For the host country, foreign equity investment has the potential of providing a substantial new source of capital. Many corporations in developing countries have outgrown their existing domestic equity markets. Access by foreign investors would alleviate the high corporate debt-to-equity ratios found in many developing countries while stimulating local investor activity. Despite these potential benefits, many Third World countries maintain tight restrictions on foreign portfolio investment.

These restrictions and the inadequate development of Third World financial markets are major deterrents to inflows of equity investment.

Market Structure. Many developing countries have no stock market. And where a stock market exists, turnover and liquidity are low, and regulation is rudimentary. Rarely does an institution like the Securities and Exchange Commission exist to require adequate disclosure of company information and to protect investors. Insider trading and speculation often result in unstable prices.

Despite this general picture, some countries have been making efforts to improve and strengthen their securities markets. Hong Kong has established a security commission with strong regulatory powers. In recent years, Mexico has increased the power of the Comision Nacional de Valores, which is now an effective supervisory organization. In July 1983, Korea passed legislation that has strengthened and stabilized its stock market. According to Antoine van Agtmael, "Accounting, auditing and disclosure standards in the fifteen largest emerging markets are adequate and comparable, in most cases, to European standards."[37]

Lack of liquidity is a major deterrent to foreign investment in many Third World stock markets. Typically, only the few stocks of the largest corporations are actively traded. Most companies are privately owned and therefore not listed on the stock exchange. Several developing countries have adopted measures in recent years to encourage firms to go public. Reduction in the corporate tax has had such an effect in Indonesia, Thailand, Egypt, and Korea. Recently, two major Korean companies, Samsung Semiconducters and Hyundai Engineering and Construction, became public corporations and are now listed on the Korean exchange. The encouragement of privately owned companies to go public is a welcome development.

Restrictions. Even in countries with fairly well-developed stock markets, the policy environment may not be conducive to attracting international equity investment. Common barriers are exchange restrictions on foreign equity investment, discriminatory treatment of foreign investors, capital gains taxes, high withholding taxes on dividend income, minimum periods during which foreign funds must remain invested, and restrictions on the types and amounts of shares that can be purchased or held by foreign investors.

Investment Funds. Countries that restrict or prohibit direct foreign equity investment in their domestic companies may permit the establishment of mutual funds as vehicles for the investment of foreign capital in domestic securities. The shares of closed-end funds may be traded on the major stock exchanges of the industrial countries. One of the benefits for the issuing country is that shares sold by a foreign investor are likely to be bought by another foreign investor, thus obviating the need for the country of origin to supply foreign exchange; only the payment of dividends requires the country to use foreign exchange.

In contrast, open-end funds are not traded on the world securities markets. Instead, the fund manager buys and sells stocks in the local market in response to net deposits to or withdrawals from the fund. Whenever there is a net foreign withdrawal, the country experiences a foreign exchange loss. Therefore, this form of mutual fund can be used only by a country that does not have foreign exchange controls. Some funds are, consequently, semi-open-end funds. They operate as open-end funds with stipulation that they may become closed-end funds if the government imposes exchange controls.

Korea has three investment funds. Two are semi-open-end mutual funds operating in the Euromarket; the other is a closed-end fund listed on the New York Stock Exchange. All three funds were created with the aid of the IFC. Mexico has a closed-end fund listed on both the New York and the London exchanges. Taiwan, Thailand, and Brazil also operate mutual funds. One of the advantages of Latin American funds is that they might serve as attractive vehicles for the repatriation of flight capital to the home country.

In 1971, the IFC established its Capital Markets Department, which has become the focal point of IFC and World Bank financial development activities. Since then, the IFC has taken an active role in promoting the development of stock markets in the Third World and encouraging their openness to foreigners. It has recently developed a plan to launch a $50 million closed-end fund that would include stocks from a wide range of developing countries. Initially, participation would be limited to about ten institutional investors from the industrialized countries. The aim of the fund is to demonstrate the attractiveness of investing in Third World stocks. Eventually, the IFC hopes to develop the enterprise into a $500 million fund in which the typical investors would be small and medium-sized financial institutions that seek geographic distribution in emerging markets.[38]

In order to benefit from foreign equity capital, developing countries should phase out their restrictions on this form of investment. They should concentrate their efforts on regulation and oversight of their securities markets while avoiding discriminatory restrictions on foreign investors.

Developing countries are increasingly realizing that a well-functioning securities market can also play an important role in domestic finance by contributing to mobilizing domestic savings, stimulating a more efficient allocation of investment, reducing concentration of ownership, and improving the accounting and auditing standards of private business. We strongly endorse the work of the IFC in aiding in the creation and support of institutions in Third World countries that contribute to the growth and improvement of indigenous capital markets.

Outlook

The primary obstacles to a larger flow of portfolio equity capital are sluggish growth and political instability in many developing countries. However, even with improved general conditions abroad, the potential for such investment can be realized only if restrictions are removed and institutional improvements are made in domestic capital markets.

Given the undeveloped nature of most Third World securities markets, it is unlikely that foreign equity investment will be substantial enough in the near future to contribute significantly to the development of more than a select group of the more advanced developing countries. For the majority of the developing countries, levels of foreign equity investment are likely to remain insignificant for the next decade, and those countries will continue to rely on more traditional means of development financing.

6

Commercial Lending

During the 1972–1982 period, private lending through international financial channels became the largest source of external capital for developing countries, far exceeding the volume of official development assistance or private direct investment. This flow, averaging $60 billion annually between 1979 and 1981, occurred largely in the form of commercial bank lending but also included about $2 billion of suppliers' credits and $1 billion of international bond issues.

Commercial lending on this scale would have been unimaginable twenty-five years ago. At that time, the amount was less than 10 percent of the recent volume and accounted for only a small share of total flows of capital to developing countries. Moreover, the great bulk of commercial lending in recent years has been directly to governments and public entities or in the form of publicly guaranteed loans.

The cumulation of Third World external borrowing from private and official sources resulted in an estimated outstanding international indebtedness in 1985 of $950 billion.[1] In many ways, this massive flow of capital represented a remarkable success, having contributed to sustaining high rates of growth in real output in the developing world under the adverse conditions of the 1970s, including two oil price shocks and slow growth in the industrial countries.[2]

However, developments of the past four years have raised serious questions about the scale and character of resource transfers through commercial lending that evolved in the 1970s. More than fifty debt reschedulings[3] and numerous arrears and moratoriums bear witness to the inability of many countries to service their debts in accordance with the original terms. Attempts to restore creditworthiness following repayment difficulties have typically required severe economic austerity in the borrowing country at a high cost in political, social, and economic terms.

As a result of the Third World debt problems, private international lending has fallen off sharply, and much of the flow that has occurred since 1982 has been *involuntary* bank lending under the aegis of the IMF. Despite the many problems, developing countries will need a continuing net inflow of private loan capital to regain their growth momentum and sustain it over the long run. For this to happen, however, the lessons of the debt crisis will need to be reflected first and foremost in improved domestic policies in debtor countries but also in a healthier world economic environment, modifications in commercial lending practices, and strengthened roles for the IMF and the World Bank.

Promising possibilities exist for improving the present system of commercial lending, including the further development of a secondary market for bank loans, cash-flow matching, and the creation of private insurance facilities. Moreover, as their creditworthiness improves, the developing countries will have greater access to the international securities market, whose role in private international lending has been increasing relative to that of commercial bank lending.

Evolution of Private Lending

In response to the changing requirements of borrowers and lenders, commercial lending to developing countries has gone through three broad stages in the post-World War II period: before 1974; 1974 to 1982; and since 1982.

Before 1974

It is commonly believed that bank lending to developing countries on a significant scale originated with the recycling of oil surpluses following the first oil price shock of 1973–1974. Actually, a rapid expansion of the role of private banks in the financing of developing countries took place in the late 1960s and early 1970s. This phenomenon was associated with three major developments during that period: the growth of the Euromarkets and international banking more generally; the emergence of a growing number of economically successful and creditworthy developing country borrowers; and the improvement in the terms of trade of many developing countries culminating in the 1972–1973 commodity price boom.[4]

During the late 1960s and early 1970s, bank lending to developing countries was part of the ongoing process of transferring excess savings from the high-income industrial countries (reflected in a combined current-account surplus) to the developing countries. With relatively low per capita incomes, many developing countries were unable to generate sufficient domestic savings to match domestic investment opportunities. Borrowing from private banks provided the supplementary financial means to acquire real resources from the industrial countries beyond what was available through the traditional flows of official development assistance and direct investment. By the time of the first oil shock, bank lending to developing countries had reached an annual flow of $10 billion and helped to finance current-account deficits ranging between 1 and 3 percent of GDP for the oil-importing developing countries as a whole.[5]

1974 to 1982

The traditional patterns of world payments imbalances and corresponding international capital flows were radically changed between 1974 and 1981. With the drastic increases in oil prices in 1974 and again in 1979, the combined savings of the industrial countries fell sharply in relation to their domestic investment. This change was reflected in a curtailment in the net flow of their own financial resources into international channels. During the entire period, net outflows of capital absorbed only about three-quarters of a percent of the national savings of the industrial countries, compared with about 2 1/2 percent during the preceding six years.[6]

At the same time, however, major new sources of funds were generated in the oil-exporting countries in the form of surpluses of foreign exchange beyond what they spent on current imports. This drastic change in the structure of current-account balances is shown in Table 17. Indirectly, through the recycling process, the surpluses of the oil-exporting countries became the principal source of external capital for the non-oil-exporting developing countries.

After the first oil price increase, about 50 percent of the OPEC surplus was placed in bank deposits, mainly in the Eurocurrency markets. This figure reached 61 percent after the second price rise. In each instance, OPEC members then gradually deployed a larger percentage of their surplus in higher-yielding, less liquid assets, including government and corporate securities, real estate, and direct investments. Approximately 40 percent of the cumulative OPEC surplus was placed in the United States and the United Kingdom, countries with deep and well-functioning financial markets. Substantial amounts were also placed in France, Germany, Japan, and Switzerland.

The expansion of bank liquidity during this period coincided with a reduction or abolition of controls on international capital flows and a relaxed regulatory environment. At the same time, the attitude of banks toward lending to developing countries became more favorable. Because economic growth in many of the newly industrializing countries during the 1970s greatly outpaced the performance of the industrial countries, the banks regarded the returns on lending to them as high compared with the risks.

Table 17

Current-Account Balances of Industrial and Developing Countries, 1970 to 1984
(billions of dollars)

Country Group	1970–1972[a]	1973	1974	1975–1978[a]	1979	1980	1981	1982	1983	1984
Industrial countries	7.0	10.3	-14.6	12.1	-5.6	-38.8	3.1	1.2	2.2	-34.2
United States	0.4	9.1	7.6	1.2	2.6	6.6	10.7	-3.8	-35.5	-93.4
Other six large industrial countries	9.3	0.6	-10.4	19.0	4.6	-18.7	8.8	17.7	39.0	53.2
Middle Eastern oil exporters	2.0	6.5	55.9	33.8	61.9	99.6	56.3	3.3	-11.1	-6.0
Developing countries[b]	-12.8	-9.1	-21.0	-39.5	-51.7	-68.0	-105.1	-99.2	-56.7	-35.6

Note: World total does not equal zero because of measurement errors and incomplete coverage.

[a] Annual average.
[b] Based on a sample of ninety developing countries.

Source: World Bank, <u>World Development Report 1985</u>, p. 33.

The developing countries, in turn, were attracted to bank lending during the 1970s by a number of features of that form of finance. Much of bank lending was for general purposes rather than for specific projects. It was also usually free from the conditionality attached to official finance and from the comparatively strict creditworthiness standards of bond markets.

> From the standpoint of a developing country, a Eurobank is a wonderful institution. It takes two years to borrow from the World Bank, which rightly demands expensive feasibility studies, asks hundreds of questions, brings in large, time-consuming teams on innumerable visits, and issues mountains of paper, whereas one can borrow from a Eurobank in a few weeks, on the basis of conversations and letters. This flexibility has special value because it means that new borrowing can be used to repay old borrowing, which is one of the conditions for a high debt ratio to be tolerable when the loans are not repaying themselves.[7]

In addition, real interest rates remained low or negative from 1974 to the end of the decade. By 1981, annual medium- and long-term net commercial lending to developing countries reached a peak of more than $60 billion and helped to finance a combined current-account deficit of $106 billion, an amount equivalent to approximately 5 percent of the GDP of developing countries.

Since 1982

Even in 1981, the peak year of commercial lending to developing countries, the main source of the loanable funds was shrinking rapidly. The current-account surplus of the Middle Eastern oil exporters declined from $100 billion in 1980 to $56 billion in 1981; and by 1982, it had virtually disappeared (see Table 17). After 1982, the combined current account of the oil exporters turned negative, converting that group of countries from net international lenders to net borrowers. The radical shift in the balance of payments of the oil-exporting countries has been one of the main factors tending to tighten the supply of international credit in the 1980s.

Signs of strain in the system were becoming apparent even before 1982, when the Mexican financial crisis erupted. World recession had a sharply adverse effect on developing countries' exports, and their ability to service their huge debts was further weakened by the second oil shock and the sharp rise in real interest rates. By 1982–1983, the debt problem became widespread, with all three of the Third World's largest debtors (Brazil, Mexico, and Argentina) forced to suspend normal debt servicing and enter into arrangements for formal reschedulings.

The deterioration in the creditworthiness of developing countries meant a reduced willingness on the part of the banks to increase their exposure. At the same time, bank regulators began to monitor liquidity and solvency ratios more closely and to urge banks to diversify their portfolios and to set more funds aside in loan-loss reserves. The more cautious attitudes of the banks and the regulators were reinforced by the emergence of more profitable opportunities for lending within industrial countries as the economic recovery gathered steam.

A further cause of the diminution in international bank lending is the change in the structure of world payments imbalances. The pattern in the 1970s consisted essentially of OPEC surpluses, with their counterpart in developing country deficits. The major imbalance in the world economy in the 1980s is the huge current-account deficit of the United States (averaging more than $100 billion in 1984 and 1985) financed in large part by the surpluses of Japan and Germany. Whereas the deficits of the developing countries were financed primarily through the intermediation of the banks, the U.S. deficit has been financed more by the sale of financial assets, chiefly Treasury securities. Because of the depth and efficiency of its financial markets, this has been a feasible option for the United States but not generally for developing countries. Thus, most developing countries remain dependent on bank finance while the international intermediation process has been shifting from banks to asset markets.

All these factors are reflected in the sharp decline in net bank lending to developing countries after 1981 both in absolute terms and in relation to other sources of financing for their current-account deficits. As shown in Table 7, bank lending to the indebted developing countries (including all developing countries except the Middle East oil exporters) declined from $82.4 billion in 1981 to $16.5 billion in 1983. Most of the net bank lending that *is* taking place is currently going to the developing countries of East Asia.[8] Over the same period, the flows of other types of resources (official finance and direct investment) either stagnated or declined.

Dimensions and Structure of External Debt

Growth of Debt

Net borrowing over the past fifteen years has resulted in a rapid rise in cumulative external debt. As recorded in the World Bank's Debtor Reporting System (DRS), long-term debt (maturity of over one year) increased more than tenfold, from $68 billion to $711 billion, over the 1970–1985 period (see Table 18). This represents an average annual rise

Table 18

Debt Indicators for all Developing Countries in Selected Years, 1970 to 1985
(percent)

	1970	1974	1976	1978	1980	1981	1982	1983	1984	1985
Ratio of debt to GNP	14.1	15.4	18.1	21.0	21.1	22.8	26.8	31.8	32.7	33.0
Ratio of debt to exports	108.9	80.0	100.2	113.1	90.1	97.5	116.4	134.3	130.4	135.7
Debt-service ratio	14.7	11.8	13.6	18.4	16.1	17.7	20.7	19.4	19.8	21.9
Ratio of interest service to GNP	0.5	0.8	0.8	1.1	1.6	1.9	2.4	2.4	2.6	2.7
Total debt outstanding and disbursed (billions)	$68	$141	$204	$313	$432	$493	$552	$630	$674	$711
Private sources of debt as percentage of total	50.9	56.5	59.0	61.5	63.3	64.5	64.9	66.1	65.7	64.5

Note: Data are based on a sample of ninety developing countries.

Source: World Bank, World Development Report 1985, p. 24, Table 2.6, and World Development Report 1986, p. 32, Table 2.11.

of 16.9 percent. Total external liabilities of all developing countries, including countries not reporting to the DRS as well as short-term debt and borrowings from the IMF, were estimated at $950 billion in 1985 (see Table 19).

Actually, the more than tenfold increase in debt between 1970 and 1985 is less startling than the nominal figures indicate. By relating the debt to changes in nominal GNP, both inflation and the real growth of GNP in the developing countries are taken into account. On that basis, the rise in the debt burden is much more modest: from 14.1 percent of GNP in 1970 to 33 percent in 1985 for all developing countries. Moreover, because exports have risen more rapidly than GNP,[9] the ratio of external debt to exports has risen considerably more slowly than the ratio of debt to GNP: from 108.9 in 1970 to 135.7 in 1985 (see Table 18).

Debt Service

When debt service (interest and amortization) rather than the debt itself is taken into consideration, the comfort provided by the growth of exports is somewhat reduced. Primarily because of rising interest rates, debt service has increased more rapidly than the outstanding debt: from 14.7 percent of exports in 1970 to 21.9 in 1985. Over this period, interest payments increased from one-third of total debt service to over one-half, reflecting both the increased volume of debt and the higher level of interest rates (see "The Burden of Debt").

Some of the increase in the debt-service ratio,[10] at least until 1980, reflected the larger inflation component of interest rates. Because inflation erodes the real value of the principal, the higher interest rate includes an inflation adjustment not only for the nominal interest rate but also to offset the fall in the real value of the principal that has to be repaid eventually. In effect, therefore, high interest rates attributable to inflation have included a component representing an acceleration of the amortization of the principal in real terms. However, by 1981–1982, inflation was declining, but nominal interest rates remained high, thus increasing the real debt-service burden.

Distribution of Debt by Borrowers and Lenders

Developing country debt is unevenly distributed. More than two-thirds has been borrowed by countries in the Western Hemisphere and Asia (see Table 20). Within those regions, more than 60 percent is concentrated in just seven countries classified by the IMF as "major borrowers": Brazil, Mexico, Argentina, Venezuela, Korea, Indonesia, and the Philippines (see Table 21).

The Burden of Debt

A useful general criterion for determining whether a country's burden of debt is improving or deteriorating is the relationship between the growth of its export earnings and the interest rate. If a country's current account (excluding interest) is in balance, its debt will grow by the amount of past debt multiplied by the interest rate. If the ratio of debt to exports is to be kept from increasing, exports must grow at least at the same rate.

Applying this criterion to the experience of the developing countries illuminates the onset of the Third World debt crisis. Except for 1975, the rate of growth of exports exceeded the interest rate (the London interbank offer rate, or LIBOR, plus 1 percent) by a wide margin during the 1973–1980 period. However, this relationship was sharply reversed when the world plunged into recession in 1981–1982. Interest rates rose to a postwar record while the growth of Third World exports dropped in 1980 and 1981 and actually turned negative in 1981 and 1982.[a] Thus, as shown in Table 18, the debt burden of the developing countries as reflected in the debt-to-exports ratio was lower in 1980 than in 1970, but it increased steeply in subsequent years.

So long as export growth remains below the rate of interest, the burden of debt must grow unless a country achieves a trade surplus.[b] If a country is running a trade surplus, at least part of its interest obligation on accumulated debt is being financed from current export earnings rather than from new borrowings. In this situation, debt does not automatically increase at the interest rate, and a reduction in the debt burden is consistent with more modest export growth.

It is not unreasonable to expect countries that are already heavily in debt to try to improve their creditworthiness by running trade surpluses. A positive trade balance would reduce the ratio of debt to exports until such time as more sustainable ratios are achieved. This does not imply that the country needs to reduce its outstanding debt but only that the increase should be proportionately less than the increase in exports. To the extent that interest rates exceed the growth of developing country exports, there is no way that a country can reduce its ratio of debt to exports except by running a trade surplus.

[a]William R. Cline, *International Debt: Systemic Risk and Policy Response* (Washington, D.C.: Institute for International Economics, 1984), p. 6.

[b]In this context, the term *trade surplus* is used as shorthand for a surplus in the current account excluding interest.

Moreover, almost 80 percent of the long-term debt of the major borrowers is owed to private creditors. Loans from private creditors tend to be not only at higher interest rates than borrowings from official sources but also for shorter terms. Because loans from private sources were the fastest-growing component of Third World debt, the average maturity of long-term debt fell from 20.5 years in 1970 to 13.9 years in 1982. In 1983, the average maturity and grace periods for new loans were the shortest on record for developing countries, but some improvement occurred in 1984.

On the other hand, low-income countries (such as India, Sri Lanka, Tanzania, and Egypt) receive much of their capital inflows in low-interest, long-maturity loans from official sources. For countries in this category,

Table 19

External Liabilities of Developing Countries, 1980 to 1986
(billions of dollars)

Country Group	1980	1981	1982	1983	1984[a]	1985[b]	1986[b]
DRS reporting countries[c]	570	662	737	793	828	865	920
Long-term debt[d,e]	427	490	547	622	665	708	755
From official sources	161	177	195	215	232	250	273
From private sources[e]	266	313	352	407	433	458	482
Short-term debt[e,f]	134	158	170	140	129	120	165
Use of IMF credit[g]	9	14	20	30	33	37	
Other developing countries[h]	62	67	72	78	80	85	90
Long-term debt[d]	44	43	46	52	52	56	60
From official sources	14	16	19	20	23	24	26
From private sources	30	27	27	32	30	32	34
Short-term debt[f]	18	23	25	25	27	28	30
Use of IMF credit[g]	0	1	1	1	1	1	
Total	632	729	809	871	908	950	1,010
Growth of total liabilities (%)	-	15.3	11.0	7.7	4.2	4.6	6.3

[a] Data for 1984 are preliminary.

[b] Date for 1985 are estimated and for 1986 are projected.

[c] Includes data for 107 developing countries for which standard and complete reporting is made through the World Bank's Debtor Reporting System (DRS).

[d] Debt of original maturity of more than one year.

[e] Data reflect the known rescheduling of some $40 billion of short-term debt to banks into long-term debt in 1983-1985.

[f] Debt of original maturity no more than one year. Data are estimated from information on bank claims on developing countries as reported by the BIS and are amended to take account of information on short-term debt reported by individual developing countries.

[g] Excludes loans from the IMF Trust Fund; they are included in long-term debt.

[h] Includes data for developing countries that do not report through the DRS, and for those that either have reported incomplete data through the DRS or report in a form that does not admit publication in the standard tables. Excludes debt of the high-income oil-exporting countries, and includes estimates for developing countries that are not World Bank members but are included in the global analysis underlying the <u>World Development Report</u>.

Source: World Bank, <u>World Debt Tables 1985-86</u>, p. xi.

Table 20

Indebted Developing Countries, by Region: External Debt, by Class of Creditor, End of Year, 1977 to 1986*
(billions of dollars)

	1977	1978	1979	1980	1981	1982	1983	1984	1985	1986
INDEBTED DEVELOPING COUNTRIES										
Total debt	**332.4**	**398.3**	**470.9**	**565.0**	**660.5**	**747.0**	**790.7**	**827.7**	**865.3**	**896.5**
Short term	63.2	71.9	81.8	113.3	136.2	154.6	137.3	126.3	104.9	107.3
Long term	269.2	326.5	389.1	451.7	524.3	592.4	653.4	701.3	760.3	789.2
Unguaranteed[a]	55.1	57.8	68.7	83.0	104.4	114.2	108.8	110.5	104.1	102.5
Guaranteed[a]	214.1	268.7	320.4	368.7	419.9	478.2	544.6	590.8	656.3	686.7
To official creditors	109.7	130.8	149.1	172.4	192.8	218.6	243.0	266.4	295.2	314.6
To financial institutions	72.9	99.6	130.2	154.0	182.1	208.5	249.8	271.2	304.1	313.4
To other private creditors	31.5	38.3	41.1	42.3	45.0	51.1	51.8	53.2	56.9	58.7
By region										
Africa										
Total debt	**60.9**	**72.2**	**84.0**	**94.1**	**102.8**	**117.2**	**123.3**	**126.8**	**130.0**	**131.5**
Short term	12.2	9.0	8.7	10.4	13.2	16.8	20.2	18.3	17.7	17.4
Long term	48.8	63.2	75.3	83.7	89.6	100.4	103.1	108.5	112.3	114.0
To official creditors	19.2	23.9	30.1	36.0	41.1	49.3	53.2	57.8	62.1	65.0
To financial institutions[b]	15.7	22.6	27.7	29.7	31.2	34.8	33.8	34.1	33.4	31.9
To other private creditors[c]	13.9	16.7	17.6	18.0	17.4	16.4	16.0	16.6	16.9	17.1
Asia										
Total debt	**83.4**	**93.8**	**110.2**	**134.3**	**155.0**	**179.8**	**197.1**	**210.9**	**230.9**	**250.1**
Short term	14.2	15.8	20.3	27.0	30.2	35.7	35.6	34.2	29.9	29.9
Long term	69.2	78.0	89.9	107.2	124.8	144.1	161.5	176.7	201.1	220.3
To official creditors	44.6	51.2	55.4	62.8	70.2	77.7	85.2	93.1	104.7	113.8
To financial institutions[b]	9.7	12.5	18.5	24.4	29.8	36.8	43.4	48.4	56.4	63.8
To other private creditors[c]	14.9	14.3	16.0	20.0	24.8	29.5	33.0	35.2	40.0	42.7

Europe										
Total debt	**38.2**	**47.3**	**55.3**	**67.0**	**71.5**	**72.7**	**75.3**	**79.1**	**81.4**	**82.2**
Short term	11.1	14.2	11.8	13.5	13.6	12.0	11.6	12.0	13.7	14.6
Long term	27.1	33.1	43.5	53.6	57.9	60.7	63.7	67.1	67.7	67.6
To official creditors	10.2	13.3	14.5	17.9	19.9	22.0	22.5	24.3	24.5	24.3
To financial institutions[b]	7.7	9.6	14.8	18.4	20.7	20.9	23.5	26.1	27.3	28.4
To other private creditors[c]	9.1	10.2	14.2	17.3	17.3	17.8	17.7	16.7	15.8	14.9
Non-oil Middle East										
Total debt	**25.8**	**30.7**	**36.3**	**41.9**	**46.8**	**52.0**	**56.0**	**59.7**	**65.8**	**69.1**
Short term	5.6	6.1	7.0	9.1	10.5	11.3	12.6	13.9	15.2	16.4
Long term	20.2	24.7	29.3	32.8	36.3	40.7	43.5	45.8	50.6	52.7
To official creditors	14.0	17.6	21.5	24.2	26.4	29.7	31.5	34.3	38.7	40.5
To financial institutions[b]	2.0	2.5	2.5	2.6	2.8	3.2	3.5	3.5	3.5	3.6
To other private creditors[c]	4.1	4.6	5.3	6.0	7.1	7.8	8.5	8.1	8.4	8.6
Western Hemisphere										
Total debt	**124.1**	**154.4**	**185.2**	**227.8**	**284.3**	**325.3**	**338.9**	**351.1**	**357.1**	**363.6**
Short term	20.1	26.8	34.0	53.4	68.7	78.8	57.3	47.9	28.4	29.0
Long term	104.0	127.6	131.2	174.4	215.6	246.5	281.6	303.2	328.7	334.6
To official creditors	21.7	24.8	27.5	31.5	35.2	40.0	50.6	56.9	65.3	71.1
To financial institutions[b]	37.7	52.4	66.8	78.9	97.5	112.8	145.6	159.1	183.5	185.7
To other private creditors[c]	44.5	50.4	56.9	64.0	82.9	93.8	85.4	87.2	79.9	77.8

* Excludes debt owed to the Fund. For classification of countries in groups shown here, see the Introduction to this appendix.

[a] By an official agency of the debtor country.

[b] Covers only public and publicly guaranteed debt.

[c] Includes all unguaranteed debt on the presumption that this is owed mainly to private creditors.

Source: IMF, World Economic Outlook, April 1985, Appendix Table 45.

Table 21

Indebted Developing Countries, by Financial Criteria, External Debt, by Class of Creditor, End of Year, 1977 to 1986*
(billions of dollars)

	1977	1978	1979	1980	1981	1982	1983	1984	1985	1986
MARKET BORROWERS										
Total debt	**219.6**	**265.9**	**314.5**	**382.8**	**460.8**	**528.9**	**547.1**	**575.7**	**593.1**	**608.2**
Short term	46.1	52.0	61.6	90.9	112.9	130.6	112.6	99.2	75.5	76.0
Long term	173.5	214.0	252.9	291.9	347.8	396.3	444.4	476.5	517.6	532.2
To official creditors	41.5	49.7	54.6	61.3	67.6	77.9	92.0	101.4	115.5	123.5
To financial institutions[a]	60.0	83.3	105.2	124.4	151.1	176.4	215.3	235.6	267.0	274.4
To other private creditors[b]	72.0	80.9	93.2	106.2	129.1	144.0	137.2	139.5	135.2	134.4

Of which:										
Major borrowers										
Total debt	**128.6**	**159.6**	**191.2**	**235.8**	**290.2**	**336.4**	**351.0**	**360.2**	**369.3**	**377.4**
Short term	25.5	33.1	42.7	66.3	82.8	97.3	77.4	68.0	44.2	44.5
Long term	103.1	126.5	148.5	169.5	207.4	239.1	273.6	292.2	325.1	332.9
To official creditors	22.7	27.1	29.2	32.3	36.5	41.3	49.7	55.1	65.4	70.5
To financial institutions[a]	36.0	50.8	65.2	77.8	97.1	113.0	143.6	152.7	178.7	181.0
To other private creditors[b]	44.3	48.7	54.1	59.3	73.8	84.8	80.3	84.4	81.0	81.4
Official borrowers										
Total debt	**37.6**	**43.7**	**50.8**	**61.0**	**69.1**	**78.3**	**85.3**	**93.5**	**101.7**	**110.0**
Short term	1.6	1.8	2.0	3.5	3.9	4.6	4.4	5.1	5.6	6.0
Long term	36.0	41.9	48.8	57.5	65.2	73.6	80.9	88.4	96.1	103.9
To official creditors	27.1	32.1	38.8	47.1	54.5	62.4	68.7	76.0	83.2	90.7
To financial institutions[a]	4.4	5.4	6.2	6.6	7.1	7.6	8.7	8.5	9.1	9.3
To other private creditors[b]	4.5	4.3	3.7	3.8	3.6	3.6	3.6	3.8	3.8	3.9

* By an official agency of the debtor country.

[a] Covers only public and publicly guaranteed debt.

[b] Includes all unguaranteed debt on the presumption that this is owed mainly to private creditors.

Source: IMF, World Economic Outlook, April 1985, Appendix Table 46.

debt-service ratios tend to be low even when the ratio of debt to GNP or to exports may be high.

Other Features of Debt Structure

Two other changes in the debt structure of developing countries also contributed to their financial instability. One was the rise in the share of floating-rate debt from 16 percent of the total debt in 1974 to 43 percent in 1984. The increase was concentrated among the middle-income countries, especially in Latin America. The second was the rise in the share of public and publicly guaranteed debt denominated in dollars. In 1983, the ratio was 80 percent. The increase in the foreign exchange value of the dollar between 1980 and 1985 meant higher debt-service costs in terms of domestic goods. At the same time, it tended to depress the dollar prices of commodities and therefore the dollar value of exports from developing countries, particularly those heavily dependent on primary product exports. About two-fifths of the increase in the debt-service ratio of developing countries was due to these factors.[11]

Because of the diversity of the economic situation in individual countries, standard debt indicators need to be used with caution. For example, the most widely used guide to a country's debt problems is the debt-service ratio. Low-income Latin American countries have had lower debt-service ratios than middle-income Latin American countries. This might suggest that African countries are in less serious economic and financial difficulties, but the opposite is the case. Poor and inflexible economies may be more vulnerable than others with higher debt-service ratios but a greater margin of resources and institutional capacity to take corrective action when growth and exports are threatened.

Resource Transfers

A number of the most indebted developing countries have recently been trying to improve their creditworthiness by running trade surpluses. In the lexicon of the World Bank, when a developing country runs a trade surplus, it is experiencing *negative resource transfers* (i.e., it is shipping out of the country more resources in the form of exports than it is bringing in in form of imports). This terminology also reflects the fact that a trade surplus implies that net inflows of capital are less than outflows of interest payments. It also has the unfortunate connotation that developing countries are unjustly paying out more than they are taking in even when they continue to be net importers of capital.

It would make more economic sense to define net transfers in terms of the complete current account (i.e., including rather than excluding interest). After all, interest is paid for the use of capital in the same way that rent is paid for the use of buildings or trucks, premiums are paid for insurance, and fees are paid for technological services. When all services, including the services of capital borrowed abroad, are included in imports, net transfers of goods and services are positive for the developing countries. This inward transfer of resources is the counterpart of the deficit on the current account now being experienced by all categories of developing countries.[12] To the extent that the inward transfer takes the form of non-debt-creating flows such as foreign direct investment or official grants, the debt-servicing burden of recipient countries is relieved.

In reaction to the debt crisis, many of the most indebted developing countries adopted austerity measures resulting in a sharp compression of imports and a severe slowdown in growth. As a result, substantial trade surpluses were achieved in 1983 even though exports failed to increase or rose only modestly. However, as the world economic recovery gathered force in 1984, Third World exports increased substantially, pulled up by expanding demand in the industrial countries. The trade surpluses achieved in 1984 helped to utilize idle capacity and revive the economies of a number of the indebted countries. Nevertheless, widespread economic strain and debt-servicing difficulties have persisted, necessitating continuing moratoriums and rescheduling operations.

Lessons of Debt Problem

Given the long-term focus of this policy statement, we do not deal specifically with the numerous proposals for resolving the current debt problem, which range from sweeping plans for new institutions to buy up developing country debt at a discount, to more pragmatic and flexible case-by-case approaches. Included among the latter are adjustment programs by borrowing countries under the aegis of the IMF and the World Bank, the stretch-out of repayments, and some net new lending by commercial banks. It is nevertheless necessary to examine the causes of the debt problem and try to identify the lessons to be drawn from it if private lending is again to play an important (though less dominant) role in intermediating capital transfers to the developing countries over the long run. The causes fall into three broad categories: the economic policies of the borrowing countries; world economic development; and the lending practices of the commercial banks.

Policies of Developing Countries

Domestic economic policies are the fundamental determinant of the economic performance of developing countries, the effectiveness of their use of foreign capital, and their capacity to service their external debts. However, shortcomings of domestic policies are by no means the only cause of recent debt-servicing problems. Even with sound economic policies, countries have had extreme difficulties in coping with the severity of the external shocks experienced in the late 1970s and early 1980s (high oil prices, steeply rising interest rates, and worldwide recession). However, flexible policies and structures based on market-determined prices and resource allocation can cushion the impact of even severe external shocks.

The essential role of foreign capital is to promote growth by permitting a country to invest more than it could if it had to rely only on national savings. In the early stages of development, when a country's capital stock is small, returns on investment are generally higher than those in mature industrial countries. Inflows of capital from abroad are therefore economically justified.

Indeed, from an idealized perspective, a developing country can be expected to go through a kind of investment life cycle. In the first stage, net borrowing exceeds the debt charge, so that even interest is paid out of new borrowing. In this stage, the country would be running a trade and current-account deficit. In the second stage, net borrowing continues but is less than the interest charge as the country's trade account moves into surplus. In the third stage, both the trade and the current accounts are in surplus, so that the amount of outstanding debt is falling. In the fourth stage, the country becomes a creditor with a net accumulation of foreign assets. In 1970, most developing countries were in stage one, but a number of them have now moved into stage two.

When a country borrows abroad, a crucial question is whether the resources are being invested economically. This means that the loan adds more to the GNP than the cost of servicing it; that the country is able to translate the additional output into foreign exchange; in the case of government borrowings, that the proceeds can also be converted into tax revenues.

Clearly, if the funds are misused, the country ends up with more foreign debt but without a corresponding increase in income from which to service it. Moreover, even if the yield from the new investment is satisfactory, the project may fail to generate or save enough foreign exchange to cover the charges on the debt. The problem may be one of timing, arising from a mismatch of loan maturity and gestation period of the projects. More fundamentally, however, the project may never be able to earn or save sufficient foreign exchange because of policy-induced distortions such as overvalued exchange rates, high protection, and various forms of subsidy. Without the distortions, it would not matter whether the investments yielded increased exports or import substitutes directly.

So long as the returns were higher than the cost of the borrowed funds, even investments in non-tradable sectors such as electricity and roads, would eventually yield increased output and savings from which an extra exportable surplus could indirectly be generated to service the debt.

The centrality of borrowing countries' policies is suggested by the differential impact of increasing debt in particular developing countries. At the risk of oversimplification, a comparison could be drawn between Korea and Mexico, two countries with roughly similar levels of per capita incomes. Each had accumulated debt in 1982 equal to about 30 percent of its GNP.[13] Confronted with the same adverse world economic situation, Korea has managed to meet its debt-servicing obligations fully and on schedule while continuing to grow at a rapid rate. Mexico, on the other hand, went into a deep financial crisis in 1982, necessitating rescue operations by the United States, the Bank for International Settlements (BIS), and the IMF. Its foreign debt had to be restructured, and severe austerity measures were adopted.[14]

Although the situation of each of the major developing country borrowers is distinctive, there appear to have been certain common and interrelated elements present in those countries experiencing the most serious debt-servicing problems: excess demand reflected in large fiscal imbalances and pressures on the balance-of-payments; capital expenditures yielding low rates of return; debt maturities too short for the gestation period of the investment; inflationary expansion of domestic credit; unrealistic exchange rates, and domestic cost-price distortions that erode international competitiveness.

In Chapter 3, we stressed the importance for developing country growth of macroeconomic and microeconomic policy reforms that address all these elements. Such reforms are particularly essential for countries whose growth is dependent on substantial inflows of foreign capital that must be serviced with foreign exchange earned by exports. The contrasting experiences of Korea and Mexico, and indeed of the East Asian and Latin American countries more broadly, is revealing in this respect. It shows that the best way to discourage the financing of low-yielding investments[15] with foreign capital is to maintain realistic exchange rates and avoid excessive protection and subsidies. Investors will then judge the true economic costs and benefits of alternative projects and direct their investments to activities in which the country has a comparative advantage in world markets. Although these policies are often politically difficult to achieve, they are required to make the best use not only of foreign capital but also of domestic resources.

Because the external economic environment is inherently uncertain, developing countries must be able to respond flexibly to change. The more a country is linked to the rest of the world through trade and capital flows, the greater its benefits but also the greater its exposure to external shocks. Borrowing countries cannot operate on the basis of the most optimistic assumptions about foreign demand and interest rates. Adverse developments are bound to occur, exerting pressure on the balance of payments. If higher levels of public spending are financed primarily by foreign borrowing rather than by increasing tax revenues, interest obligations will put cumulative strains on the budget and the balance of payments. The strains become intolerable when the external economic environment takes a downward turn.[16]

More generally, the need for foreign borrowing is dependent on the level of aggregate domestic saving and investment. The management of external debt must therefore be an integral part of macroeconomic management. Although there is no substitute for sound fiscal and monetary policies, some degree of regulation of foreign borrowing by developing countries is in order (such as limits on public borrowing and prior approval of private borrowing), particularly in countries where distorted prices, interest rates, and exchange rates could lead to overborrowing. Even without distortions, however, government approval of private borrowing is necessary when the loan is guaranteed by a public body.

Developing countries should also be encouraged to build up and maintain adequate levels of international reserves to allow adjustment to adverse external developments without jeopardizing economic growth.

World Economic Conditions

The problems created by economic mismanagement and overborrowing by developing countries were exacerbated by three major developments in the world economy over which non-oil-exporting Third World borrowers had no control: the second oil shock in 1979–1980; world economic recession in the early 1980s; and historically high real interest rates. Although the situation has markedly improved for the oil-importing developing countries, the prospects for resolving the debt problem and restoring an appropriate flow of commercial lending are being clouded by intensified protectionist pressures in the industrial countries that could lead to severe restrictions on access to their markets.

The sharp rise in the price of oil in 1979 and 1980 cost the Third World oil importers an additional $40 billion in 1981 and a similar amount in 1982. Because these sums were almost equivalent to the developing countries' total interest payments on external debt in those years,[17] they induced a massive disturbance in the international financial system.

What caused the problem was the abruptness of the price increases, which overwhelmed the internal adjustment capacities of most developing countries. More gradual increases might well have been accommodated by the developing countries, especially because the severe deflationary policy reactions in the industrial countries and their adverse effects on the developing countries might have been avoided.

Since 1982, oil prices have declined drastically from their peak of $34 per barrel for Saudi light crude. The fall was gradual until the winter of 1985–1986 when it became precipitous, reaching a trough of about $10 in the summer of 1986. Since that time there has been a partial recovery to about $18 to $20. Although the fall in oil prices from their 1982 level has benefited the oil-importing countries, it has had severe adverse effects on those developing countries that are heavily dependent on foreign exchange earnings from oil exports.

Mexico, which earns 70 percent of its foreign exchange from oil exports, has been particularly hard hit. For every $1 decline in the price of a barrel of oil, Mexico loses $550 million annually in foreign exchange (based on exports of 1.5 million barrels a day). Because of Mexico's exceptional importance to the United States in political, economic, and social terms, special measures to assist that country in overcoming its present difficulties are in order.[18]

The lower oil prices are largely due to a decade of worldwide policies of conservation and encouragement of new exploration and development. Given the long-run outlook for rising oil prices in real terms, it is essential that these policies be maintained if the risk of another oil shock is to be minimized.

The adverse direct effects of the steep rise in the price of oil in 1979–1980 on the oil-importing developing countries were greatly compounded by their indirect repercussions. The industrial countries responded to the second oil shock by tightening monetary policy in order to counter the sort of inflationary effects that had been experienced after the first oil shock. As a result, interest rates rose sharply, and a worldwide recession occurred in 1981–1982.

The contraction in real economic growth in the industrial countries was one of the most severe of the postwar period. From an average of 3.7 percent during the 1967–1979 period, real GNP growth fell to 1.4 percent in 1980–1981 and actually turned to a negative 0.1 percent in 1982.[19] As a result, commodity prices collapsed, and export volumes declined, yielding a fall in the trend rate of Third World earnings of foreign exchange.

The debt-serving strains stemming from higher oil import bills and shrinking export earnings were greatly exacerbated by the steep rise in real interest rates. The average nominal interest rate on outstanding Third World long-term debts increased from 4.5 percent in 1973–1977 to 8.5 percent in 1981–1982. Subtracting the U.S. wholesale price index, the rate rose in real terms from a negative 6 percent to a positive 3 percent. Total excess interest payments on developing country debt in 1981–1982 have been estimated at $41 billion in excess of the amounts that could have been anticipated (however unrealistically) on the basis of past real rates.[20]

In general, the combination of high real interest rates and world recession in 1981–1982 damaged the capacity of developing countries to service their debts much more than did either of the two oil price shocks taken by themselves (see Table 22). The experience of Brazil illustrates the impact on the major commercial borrowers.

> Brazil's net interest payments in 1981 were 60 percent larger than they would have been if real interest rates had remained constant, and in 1982, 80 percent larger. These increases were equivalent to 15 percent and 25 percent of actual exports in those years. At the same time, Brazil's terms of trade fell 25 percent below what might have been prudently expected in 1980. Moreover, Brazil's exports to its important markets in other developing countries suffered when they reduced their imports, and Brazil had to cut the amount of export credit it could offer.[21]

The world recovery that began in 1983 helped to ease the debt-servicing difficulties of developing countries. World GNP grew by 4.2 percent in 1984, and world trade by about 8.5 percent. As a group, the developing countries shared in this improved economic performance. Their GNP rose by 4.1 percent, and their export volume increased by 8.9 percent, compared with less than 4 percent annually in 1981 and 1982. Although real interest rates have come down, they remain at high levels.

Despite the substantial fall in the relative value of the dollar since early 1985, the recovery has not led to the normal cyclical rise in the dollar prices of most primary commodities. This is due in part to factors affecting the markets for particular primary products such as the substitution of synthetics for natural products and the expansion of supplies by subsidized state-owned mines in developing countries in the face of slack world demand. In addition, commodity prices have been affected by the weakness of the recovery in Europe.

The slowness of recovery in Europe is partly the result of tight fiscal and monetary policies, but also it reflects more deep-seated conditions that stifle investment and retard growth. Especially critical are structural rigidities in labor markets such as job protection statutes, inflexible work arrangements, and heavy social charges on employment. As a result, unemployment in the major European countries exceeds 10 percent. Essentially, there has been no net job creation in Europe since 1970,

Table 22

Impact of External Shocks on Balance of Payments in Selected Developing Countries
(average annual percentage of GNP)

Country	1974-1975	1979-1980	1981-1982
Reschedulers[a]			
Argentina	-0.6	-1.9	-6.4
Brazil	-3.7	-2.8	-8.6
Chile	-4.7	-1.2	-13.3
India	-2.6	-1.6	-4.2
Ivory Coast	0.5	-5.6	-18.9
Jamaica	-9.6	-13.3	-29.4
Mexico	-1.0	-0.2	1.0
Peru	-4.5	-1.5	-5.6
Nigeria	16.7	5.8	3.8
Morocco	0.2	-4.0	-9.7
Philippines	-6.2	-2.4	-10.1
Yugoslavia	-6.7	-2.0	-10.0
Nonreschedulers			
Colombia	-1.4	-3.6	-8.3
Kenya	-8.1	-8.7	-19.0
Egypt	-8.7	-0.8	-1.2
Tunisia	-2.1	2.7	1.9
Korea	-9.5	-8.1	-21.7
Indonesia	12.0	5.6	5.4
Tanzania	-9.3	-6.0	-14.3
Thailand	-3.7	-2.3	-10.1

Note: External shocks are defined as the impact on the balance of payments of: (a) changes in the terms of trade; (b) a decline in the growth rate of world demand for a country's exports; and (c) increases in interest rates. Data for 1974-75 show the change from 1971-73; data for 1979-80 and 1981-82 show the change from 1976-78.

[a] Countries that had rescheduled as of the end of 1984.

Source: World Bank, World Development Report 1985, Table 4.2, p. 56.

compared with the U.S. record of 26 million new jobs during the same period. Reforms in the institutional structure of European labor markets are essential.

The effects that the industrial countries will have on resolving the debt problems of the developing countries will depend heavily on what happens to economic growth, interest rates, and protectionism. Highest priority must be given to reducing the U.S. budget deficit. Although the deficit has provided some stimulus to imports from the indebted countries, this effect has been at least partially offset by the high interest rates induced by the deficit. In addition to exacerbating the debt problems of the developing countries directly, the high rates act as a depressant on world economic growth and therefore indirectly on the prospects for export expansion by the developing countries.

High real interest rates have also tended to strengthen the dollar. By increasing U.S. imports and reducing U.S. exports, the strong dollar has been a major cause of this country's unprecedented trade deficits which surpassed $120 billion in 1984 and 1985.

Although the dollar has come down substantially from its peak in early 1985, its strength has had a severe impact on the health of many U.S. industries and has ignited powerful protectionist sentiment. The rise in protectionist pressures is especially strong in sectors where comparative advantage has long been shifting to the developing countries (e.g., sugar, clothing, and shoes). In these sectors foreign competition would be intense regardless of the strength of the dollar. Moreover, the protection has usually taken the form of quantitative restrictions that directly limit the expansion of trade based on comparative costs. Perhaps as important as the immediate effect on developing country exports is the effect of protection and even the threats of protection on creating uncertainty among investors in developing countries and therefore impairing the efficiency and growth of those economies.

One of the most important tasks of public policy is to explain to the U.S. public that the solution to the problem of the trade deficit lies not in trade protection but primarily in achieving an appropriate macroeconomic policy environment in the United States and other developed countries. Protection can only shift the problem from certain industries to others.[22]

Role of the Commercial Banks

The world economic situation and the economic policies of the industrial and developing countries set the stage for the debt crisis that erupted in 1982. These factors, when combined with the massive amounts of credit supplied by the commercial banks, made a crisis unavoidable.

Much of commercial bank lending was in the form of syndicated Eurocurrency loans carrying five- to ten-year maturities and floating interest rates. Lending in this form to developing countries increased from $7 billion in 1973 to $45 billion in 1981. Collectively, Latin American countries were the biggest borrowers in the syndicated loan market. Most syndicated loans were arranged by a core of twenty-five to fifty large commercial banks in the industrial countries. Lending from this first-tier group was supplemented from time to time by loans from a second tier of almost 3,000 banks, consisting mostly of regional banks in the industrial countries but also including banks based in developing and centrally planned economies.

Encouraged by both the U.S. government and the multilateral development institutions, the large U.S. banks, with long-time customer relationships in Latin America, took the lead in international lending in the 1970s. By 1977, almost half of the total earnings of the twelve biggest U.S. banks were derived from international lending, with the bulk coming from the developing countries. The U.S. banks were then joined by British, French, and German banks and later by Japanese banks. Banks from developing countries (including Arab banks) also became increasingly active in international lending after 1977.[23]

The major borrowers among the developing countries relied on the commercial banks to finance 50 percent or more of their current-account deficits. In some cases, the borrowing approached or even exceeded the entire current-account deficit.[24] Access to large and increasing net capital inflows from commercial banks facilitated excessively expansionary macroeconomic policies, unrealistic exchange rates, and capital flight while delaying necessary adjustments.

If many of the major debtor countries can be said to have overborrowed, the commercial banks may, with hindsight, be said to have overloaned. Much of their lending was concentrated on a narrow range of countries. And for most of the period between 1977 and the early 1980s, the growth in international bank lending outstripped the growth in bank capital. In some instances, the commercial banks failed to recognize or heed early warning signs and continued to lend long after the residents of the borrowing country had themselves lost confidence in their government's policies as reflected in large-scale capital flight.[25]

Underestimation of Risk. One general reason for overlending by the banks is what two prolific writers on the subject, Guttentag and Herring, call "disaster myopia."[26] This was the tendency of banks to assign a very low probability to any major shock affecting their international loan portfolios. In the postwar era, repayment experience on international loans was relatively good in comparison with the record on domestic lending. Moreover, as the period since the last major country defaults in the 1930s lengthened, the subjective perception of the probability of such an event diminished. The prevalence of disaster myopia was reflected in the banks' willingness to lend to a single foreign country amounts equal to a major portion of their capital at spreads so narrow that any risk premiums would have had to be extremely modest. In fact, the average spreads on loans to developing countries consistently remained *below* those on large corporate loans in the United States during the 1979–1983 period.[27]

In some instances, there was also inadequate appreciation of the nature of sovereign risk. Lending to foreign governments is fundamentally different from lending to domestic borrowers. Apart from the absence of collateral, the obligation is much more difficult to enforce because a sovereign borrower may reject a claim against it within its territory. Most important, however, is the transfer risk (i.e., the risk of a decline in the ability or willingness of foreign borrowers to convert local currencies into the currency in which loans are denominated). The transfer risk is, of course, a function of the policies of the foreign government itself as they affect its external payments position. In the 1970s and 1980s, the transfer risk was amplified by the extraordinary volatility of interest rates and exchange rates. Even government-guaranteed loans to profitable foreign private business can go sour because of the inability of the private borrowers to convert local currency earnings into foreign exchange in order to service the debt.

Bank lending was also characterized by a belief that systemic risk was low. A bank with a high concentration of its capital in a developing country considered to be a good risk was reassured of the safety of its loan by the belief that a crisis in one country would not spill over to the system as a whole. The perception of systemic risk was also tempered by the belief that international institutions would act to prevent the spread of a crisis by coming to the aid of a country experiencing debt-servicing difficulties.

Difficulties in Assessing Creditworthiness. The volume and pattern of lending was affected by certain particular difficulties faced by the banks in assessing creditworthiness. Knowledge about the external debt and balance-of-payments situation of a borrowing country was rarely complete or up-to-date. Nor did banks have adequate information about amounts lent by competitor banks at the same time to the same country. To some extent, the informational problems were experienced even by the multilateral financial institutions because the governments of borrowing countries were not always fully informed about the external obligations incurred by the multiplicity of private and state-owned enterprises under their jurisdiction.

Apart from informational deficiencies, standard measures of debt-service capacity proved to be highly questionable as indicators of creditworthiness. High debt-service-ratio countries, such as Brazil and Mexico, were able to service their debts during the 1970s while some countries with much lower ratios, such as Turkey and Zaire, experienced difficulties. Attempts to develop new financial yardsticks to gauge country risk proved abortive, and banks tended to give increasing weight to subjective judgments about political and social conditions.

Tendency Toward Parallel Action. The lack of adequate data reinforced the tendency of international banks to keep their country exposures and capital ratios in line with those of other banks. This practice reduces the vulnerability of individual banks to criticism in case of a debt crisis and increases the likelihood of government assistance because the system as a whole would be at risk. Aggressive competition among some banks in lending to the developing countries, in combination with the tendency toward parallel action, led to a lowering of risk premiums and heavy concentrations of country exposure.

Fallacies of Composition. Many times, banks sought to reduce their risks by lending at floating rates and at short maturities. However, both strategies were subject to the fallacy of composition because they failed to take into account the systemic linkages among borrowers and lenders.

Floating rates appeared to transfer the interest rate risk from bank lenders to country borrowers. When a sustained increase in real interest rates occurred, however, countries that were not otherwise linked became subject to the same shock. In effect, the floating-rate policy coverted the interest rate risk on individual loans to vulnerability for the system as a whole.

Keeping loan maturities short was perceived as another precautionary strategy based on the belief that banks could reduce their exposure as debt-service difficulties loomed on the horizon. However, if a borrowing country runs a current-account deficit, a bank can reduce its exposure only if some other bank is prepared to increase its exposure or if the country is willing to liquidate some of its foreign exchange reserves or other foreign assets. With an adverse movement in the borrowing country's balance-of-payments, neither of these conditions is likely to be met. Therefore, the short-leash approach may make some creditors feel safer than they actually are and, in any case, cannot provide protection to all creditors.

Concentration of Exposure. Although the amount a bank may lend to an individual borrower within a country is limited to a fixed percentage of its capital, there are no restrictions on the total amount that can be lent to all borrowers in any one country. Among the ten largest U.S. banks, eight had loans exposures in 1982 to Mexico, Argentina, Yugoslavia, and Chile that exceeded 100 percent of their total equity.[28]

Loan concentration was encouraged by the high fixed costs incurred in developing a banking relationship with a country. This tendency was reinforced by the bargaining behavior of many country borrowers. Their continuation of a relationship became dependent less on past loans than on the willingness of the banks to extend new loans; the continued placement of deposits and purchases of services for fees became at least implicitly dependent on new lending.

Aftermath of the Debt Crisis

As the debt-service capacity of Third World borrowers became strained in 1982 by world recession and high interest rates, the weaknesses of the system of commercial bank lending became apparent. Confidence abruptly deteriorated, and new lending came to a sudden halt in the wake of Mexico's financial collapse.

In the absence of a continuing flow of credit, multiple-country defaults were threatened because the major borrowers had come to rely on new loans to pay interest on their existing debt. In these circumstances, a series of coordinated rescue operations were undertaken involving country adjustment, short-term IMF finance, official bridging loans, involuntary new lending by the commercial banks, and debt rescheduling.

Reschedulings. In orchestrating the unprecedented volume of debt-relief operations, the IMF played a central role that differed markedly from traditional practice. Prior to the 1982 crisis, a country experiencing difficulty in servicing its external debt had first to work out an economic stabilization program with the IMF. With that seal of approval, it sought to reschedule first its official debt with the so-called Paris Club of creditor governments and then its private debt with the commercial lenders. The various phases of the restructuring were essentially uncoordinated, and there was no assurance for the debtor countries of the scope and terms of their commercial negotiations.

Under the new approach, the IMF took the initiative in arranging simultaneous negotiations between individual debtor countries and all their creditors. The IMF made its own financial involvement contingent not only on the adoption of austerity programs by the debtor countries but also on the cooperation of the creditors in rescheduling the debt and providing some additional finance to assist in servicing the debt.

The IMF insistence on the link between the provision of its own funds and new lending by the commercial banks was necessitated by the *free-rider* problem. In a situation where most banks would have preferred to reduce their exposure, the major commercial banks realized the need to provide new funds to keep the borrowing countries afloat while they were taking measures to improve their debt-servicing capacity. Some of the smaller banks, however, did not want to participate in reschedulings, especially if they would be required to provide new money. By refusing to participate, they hoped to force the responsibility onto the major lending banks as well as onto public sources of funds. In this way, the smaller banks could improve the quality of their outstanding loans without having to bear any of the burden of increased exposure. The IMF strategy proved effective in dealing with this problem by giving the recalcitrant banks no alternative to bearing their fair share of new lending.

While the IMF made its own involvement contingent on the continued flow of other financing to the debtor countries, the private banks and government creditors, in turn, conditioned their financial packages on the borrowers' acceptance of the IMF programs. Thus, the IMF was reinforced in its lead role in the entire process of developing country policy reform and debt restructuring.

Despite many sweeping proposals to solve the entire debt problem at a stroke, the approach pursued under the aegis of the IMF has been on an individual-country basis. We strongly support the country-by-country approach, which takes into account the diversity of circumstances of individual debtor nations and the necessity for policy reform as an integral part of debt restructuring and new money.

Except for a few major borrowers, reschedulings have been on a year-to-year basis. Year-to-year rescheduling tends to focus on overcoming immediate financial problems rather than on dealing with underlying economic conditions affecting growth and creditworthiness. We therefore prefer multiyear rescheduling arrangements for countries that undertake credible commitments for long-term structural reform with the advice and assistance of the World Bank and the IMF.

Regulatory Changes. While the banks and the IMF were concentrating on measures to avert the financial collapse of the heavily indebted countries, the bank regulators were focusing on the need to build greater discipline and better restraints into the system of international bank lending. Their purpose was not only to prevent another crisis but to introduce more stability into the system for the long run.

The regulatory changes applying to U.S. banks were embodied in the International Lending Supervision Act of 1983, which was drawn up with the advice of the three supervising agencies: the Federal Reserve, the Federal Deposit Insurance Corporation, and the Comptroller of the Currency. By strengthening supervision, the legislation sought to discourage sovereign lending beyond limits that were prudent for the system as a whole.

The legislation contained five basic provisions. One required special reserves to be established on the outstanding claims of banks in countries experiencing debt-servicing difficulties. The *allocated transfer risk reserves* are necessary only in cases of extreme distress. To determine when such reserves would be required, the three agencies adopted a new classification system for loans adversely affected by transfer risk. In ascending order of severity, the categories are substandard, value impaired, and loss (see "Classification of Loans Adversely Affected by Transfer Risk").

Classification of Loans Adversely Affected by Transfer Risk

1. Substandard: (1) a country is not complying with its external service obligations, as evidenced by arrearages, forced restructuring, or rollovers; and (2) the country is not in the process of adopting an IMF or other suitable economic adjustment program or is not adequately adhering to such a program; or (3) the country and its bank creditors have not negotiated a viable rescheduling and are unlikely to do so in the near future.
2. Value impaired: A country has protracted arrearages, as indicated by more than one of the following: the country has not fully paid its interest for six months; the country has not complied with IMF programs (and there is no immediate prospect of compliance); the country has not met rescheduling terms for over one year; the country shows no definite prospects for an orderly restoration of debt service in the near future.
3. Loss: This category applies when the loan is considered uncollectible, and of such little value that its continuance as a bankable asset is not warranted. An example would be an outright statement by a country which repudiates obligations to banks, the IMF, or other lenders.

Source: Joint Press Release, Comptroller of the Currency, Federal Deposit Insurance Corporation, and Federal Reserve Board, *Interagency Statement on Examination Treatment of International Loans,* December 15, 1983.

Classifying a loan as substandard serves as a warning signal to banks to consider the need for setting aside reserves. However, once a loan is placed in the value-impaired category, special reserves become mandatory.[29] Such reserves are charged against current earnings and cannot be considered part of capital for the purpose of determining capital adequacy. The classification of loss means that the loan must be written off.

A second provision obliges banks to credit front-end fees on their international loans, in excess of administrative costs, over the life of the loan. The purpose is to discourage banks from taking a short-run view of the impact of international lending on their current earnings.

A third provision mandates an increase in disclosure of international loan concentrations. Banks must disclose detailed information on all exposures in a single country greater than 1 percent of their total assets or 20 percent of primary capital, whichever is less. For individual country exposures exceeding 0.75 of total assets or 15 percent of primary capital, banks are required to identify the countries and the combined exposures.[30] In an effort to keep a closer watch on changes in country exposures, banks are required to file country exposure reports quarterly rather than semiannually (the previous practice).

A fourth requirement of the 1983 act is that the supervisory agencies establish minimum levels of capital adequacy. They were also urged to take into account loan concentration levels in evaluating the capital adequacy of individual banks.

In mid-1985, the three agencies revised their guidelines on capital adequacy and established uniform minimum capital levels for all federally supervised banking organizations. The new guidelines set the minimum ratio of primary capital to total assets at 5.5 percent.[31] In general, banks have been expected to operate above the minimum levels. In order to obtain greater uniformity of capital standards internationally, efforts are currently being made to develop a weighted risk asset ratio for capital adequacy purposes.

A final provision of the act concerns international cooperation in the regulation of banks. U.S. banking agencies were instructed to consult with banking supervisors in other countries to coordinate and improve the supervision of international lending. Such consultations generally take place through the Cooke Committee, which meets under the auspices of the BIS. The United States was instrumental in establishing the committee and has been an active member since its inception in 1975. (See "The Cooke Committee and the Lender-of-Last-Resort Issue").

Remaining Issues. Several major unresolved regulatory issues remain: the legal limits for lending by U.S. banks to individual foreign countries; the tax treatment of reserves; and the recent tightening of regulatory policies.

Domestic law restricts national banks from lending more than 15 to 25 percent (depending on the type of loan) of their capital to any one borrower. Foreign individuals and enterprises have always been subject to the same lending limits that apply to domestic borrowers. However, in 1979, foreign government agencies were subjected to a means and purpose test to determine whether they were to be treated as individual borrowers or combined with the government as a single entity. To be treated as a separate borrower, the government agency had to have a means of repayment that was not dependent on general central government revenues. Also, the purpose of the loan had to be stated in the loan agreement and the proceeds used to conduct the business of the agency. No limits were established for the country as a whole.

With attention centered increasingly on transfer risk, the application of counry lending limits has gained support. Lending to foreigners is inherently different from domestic lending because of the transfer risk, which links repayment of all external loans to government actions. Although the earnings of each borrower may be separate, the need to service the loan in foreign exchange makes the government, in effect, a party to each loan contract. It has therefore been argued that legal lending limits should be applied to the country as a whole.[32]

This argument is logical in theory, but practical considerations make country lending limits undesirable. A single limit for all countries would be inappropriate because of substantial individual differences in credi-

The Cooke Committee and the Lender-of-Last-Resort Issue

The BIS Committee on Banking Regulations and Supervisory Practices, commonly known as the Cooke Committee, was created in 1975 with the objective of establishing and maintaining "close working relationships among national bank regulators to facilitate resolution of common problems and the achievment of greater coordination of approaches to bank supervision."[a]

The Committee has made progress in bringing about greater convergence of international bank regulatory and supervisory standards. However, by its nature, its work is slow and difficult. Regulatory systems and practices vary widely from country to country. The Cooke Committee is a purely consultative body and is not empowered to arrange formal agreements among its members. Policies can be adopted and implemented only at the national level.

The Committee has endorsed the principle of consolidated supervision and has sought to promote it worldwide. This means more than the acounting device of consolidating branches and subsidiaries into the accounts of parent banks; it also refers to the scope of analysis and supervisory rules. More fundamentally, consolidated supervision grows out of the principles embodied in the Concordat, which allot responsibility for solvency of the entire banking organization to the supervisor of the home country.

The question of who is the lender of last resort for subsidiaries of a foreign bank has not been addressed by the Cooke Committee. The parent country has always been regarded as responsible for branches, but no clear guidelines exist on whether the host or the parent country is responsible for subsidiaries. However, the general feeling of the members of the committee is that lender-of-last-resort responsibilities are a function of the central banks, not of the supervisors. Central banks, in turn, have deliberately left vague how they might react in certain situations, both domestically and internationally, in order to leave sufficient uncertainty in the marketplace so that institutions are not guaranteed survival.

---

[a]Charles Partee, Statement before the Subcommittee on Financial Institutions Supervision, Regulation and Insurance of the Committee on Banking, Finance and Urban Affairs, U.S. House of Representatives, in *Federal Reserve Bulletin,* May 1983, p. 344.

tworthiness. Even if the industrial countries were exempt from such a system, the large diversity in risk among developing countries would remain. According to the three regulatory agencies, "Such limits would fail to distinguish between countries capable of carrying substantial debt without significant transfer risk and countries where smaller amounts of debt still raise large transfer problems."[33]

If lending limits were to be established for each individual country, they would involve a complex system of analyzing transfer risk that would be tantamount to credit ratings. The process would undoubtedly be subject to intense political pressure from the countries involved. Transfer risk can change rapidly with shifts in government policies, but effective lending limits would have to be more stable. The international lending system could hardly function efficiently under constantly changing lending limits.

Even if country limits were a good idea, now would not be the time to impose them. Some banks have single-country exposures of over 100 percent of their equity. Among those with more conservative exposures, many would still exceed most mandated limits. Because these banks would be unable to make further loans to countries where they exceeded the legal limit, they would not be able to participate in restructurings involving involuntary lending. Even if the regulation exempted banks from the limits in cases of involuntary lending in cooperation with IMF programs, highly exposed banks would undoubtedly resist participating in involuntary lending that would further increase their country exposure. If legal lending limits were to avoid such problems, they would have to be set so high as to risk excess on the part of other banks. We therefore support the argument by the three regulatory agencies that country differences, political pressures, and the current high exposure of banks in some countries rule out country ceilings.[34]

Another unresolved issue is the tax treatment of reserves for loan losses. Recently Citicorp and a number of other banks have set aside substantial sums for this purpose. For years, transfers to the loan-loss reserve by U.S. banks received favorable tax treatment; up to 1.5 percent of the loan portfolio could be deducted from taxable income. This amount was reduced steadily in recent years to a figure of 0.6 percent. Under the new tax law, the treatment of reserves is even less favorable. It is unfortunate that the tax change comes at a time when the need to build up bank reserves is very keen and in the national interest. Implementation of the new provision should be handled in ways that do not add to the pressures on bank reserves at this time.

Bank supervisors need to walk a fine line between fulfilling their regulatory responsibilities and avoiding undue discouragement of new lending to indebted developing countries. Treasury Secretary James Baker and former Federal Reserve Chairman Paul Volcker have both stated that in appropriate circumstances, such as within the framework of the Baker Plan, new lending can improve the quality of loans already on the books by helping to restore the ability of countries to service all their external indebtedness. This principle should be borne in mind by the authorities as new regulations are considered for the treatment of developing country debt.

With more attention being given to risk analysis and capital adequacy, bank lending to developing countries will not return to the excesses of the precrisis period. Nevertheless, by strengthening the international banking system, effective supervision should contribute to a more modest and stable flow of funds to developing countries over the long run.

Table 23

New International Bond Issues and Bank Credit Commitments*
(billions of dollars)

	1981	1982	1983	1984	Jan.-Jun. 1985
International bond issues	52.8	75.5	77.1	111.5	80.1
Floating-rate notes and certificates of deposit	11.3	15.3	19.5	38.2	32.1
Fixed-rate instruments	41.5	60.2	57.6	73.3	48.0
International bank credits	147.7	103.6	80.7	117.3	44.2
Syndicated loans	94.6	98.2	67.2	62.0	25.5

* Publicly announced medium- and long-term obligations.

Source: Morgan Guaranty Trust Company, World Financial Markets, July 1985, p. 9.

Future of Bank Lending to Developing Countries

Commercial bank lenders to Third World countries have undergone a traumatic experience in the past four years. With arrears, moratoriums, and reschedulings having become virtually routine, the likelihood of any substantial early upturn in voluntary lending from present depressed levels is dim indeed. Much will depend, of course, on the extent of the improvement in Third World performance in terms of both economic growth and balance-of-payments strengthening.

Banks continue to regard themselves as overexposed in developing countries. True, their total claims on developing countries have declined in relation to their primary capital, from 287 percent in 1982, to 214 percent by the end of March 1985.[35] But the reduction in the ratio was brought about by expanding the capital base, not by reducing exposure.

Even if the economic outlook in the developing world should brighten, countries will face increasing competition for bank funds. The deregulation of U.S. financial institutions and the growth of interstate banking are opening up new domestic market opportunities for money-center banks.

Finally, the banks' role as international financial intermediaries is being constrained as some of the traditional forms of bank lending have been replaced by the issuance of securities and other marketable obligations. There has been a rapid expansion in the gross volume of new issues in the international bond market in parallel with a sharp fall in the volume of new syndicated bank loans (see Table 23). However, access to the securities markets is available only to developing countries with the highest credit ratings.

Given the adverse outlook for traditional forms of commercial bank lending to developing countries, new approaches are needed if adequate flows of private funds are to be provided in the future.

Secondary Market

One way of increasing lending while effectively disciplining the behavior of borrowers and lenders would be to develop a well-functioning secondary market for loans. Lending would increase because of the greater liquidity of loans as new participants enter the system; at the same time, the existence of reliable data on the market value of loans would exert discipline on both borrowers and lenders.

Existing Secondary Market. In recent years, a multibillion-dollar secondary market for loans to developing countries has quietly emerged. Banks have been swapping and, on a smaller scale, selling the loans, generally through intermediaries such as investment banks and other financial houses. Fees for brokering the loans have been high, reaching above 1 percent, but are coming down because of competition. The worldwide market has been substantial in absolute terms (estimated at $3 billion in 1984) but is still insignificant in relation to outstanding Third World bank debt.[36]

The emergence of a secondary market has provided considerable advantages to the participants. By selling or swapping loans, banks can adjust their portfolios for greater balance, decreasing exposure in certain countries while increasing it in others. Some U.S. banks have swapped Eastern European debt to European banks in exchange for debt of Latin American countries with which they have a greater familiarity.

Banks are not the only parties that gain from the secondary market. Debtor countries have used the market to buy their own debt at a discount. This benefits them while relieving the lender of a problem loan. Multinational corporations have also been purchasers of loans, not for investment, but as a means of acquiring local currency advantageously for their operations in a developing country. In such debt-for-equity swaps, the company buys at a discount a dollar loan made to a developing country and trades it to the central bank of that country for local currency at the full face value.

A recent constraint on the swapping of loans was a statement issued by the American Institute of Certified Public Accountants in May 1985. It recommended that, in swaps, banks should write down the value of their assets if traded below their recorded value. Previously, write-downs were necessary only if the assets were sold rather than swapped. However, this accounting change affects U.S. banks only; swaps continue to be as popular as ever with European banks.

Limitations of Secondary Markets. Although the existence of a secondary market has so far not caused difficulties, its expansion under current conditions of Third World indebtedness could create problems. The discounting of troubled loans could make it more difficult to get other banks to participate in new loans needed by borrowing countries to help service their old debts. Banks have therefore been reticent about this practice and have preferred to operate through intermediaries.

Moreover, a question arises concerning the locus of responsibility for participating in new money packages. Would it be the purchaser of the loan, or the original participant in the syndicate? Heretofore, shares in new money packages have been based on loans outstanding in 1982, making the original lender responsible. The supply of new money in concerted lending could be threatened if both buyer and seller disclaim responsibility.

A limitation on the growth of the secondary market is the restriction in the typical syndicated loan agreement on the outright sale of a loan except in the rare instance that the original agreement specifically allows it. Otherwise, the seller has to obtain the approval of the borrower and all other lenders who were party to the original agreement. Because of this restriction, most loan sales are in the form of an assignment or subparticipation that provides the purchaser with certain claims to interest and principal. However, the obligations of the borrower remain to the original lender, not the purchaser.

The growth of the secondary market for discounted loans to developing countries should not be translated into pressure on bank regulators to require that other loans to those countries on a bank's book be written down to market value.

Transferable Loan Instruments. The future functioning of a secondary market would be facilitated by the wider use of new and more flexible loan instruments. Transferable loan instruments fulfill this need by providing a vehicle for the transfer of loan commitments from a primary lender to the secondary market. When sold, such an instrument entitles the holder to receive interest and other benefits as if the holder had been the primary lender. Because transferable loan instruments can be sold in packages of varying maturities and denominations, they would be attractive to smaller banks and private investors.

Thus far, transferable loan instruments have been used only for industrial country loans, but they could be gradually extended to new finance for developing countries. They would be valuable instruments for increasing the marketability of loans to financially stable developing countries. As other countries achieved significant adjustment, this form of lending would become appropriate for them. In short, these instruments could provide the basis for the gradual development of an open and well-functioning secondary market.

Conduit System. A more formalized secondary market based on a conduit system is advocated by Guttentag and Herring.[37] Their model is the Federal Home Loan Mortgage Corporation, a quasi-government agency that has developed an efficient secondary market in home mortgages. The conduit would buy loans, pool them, and sell undivided participation interests in the entire pool. It would exercise considerable control over the market by defining eligibility requirements for the loans it would purchase and by requiring extensive financial information from a country as a condition for buying its obligations. The role of the conduit would be played by the IMF, the World Bank, or a new international agency.

We believe that a conduit system along these lines is not a practicable idea. It is doubtful that either of the existing Bretton Woods institutions would want to assume that role, and the creation of an entirely new agency is unlikely to receive much support. Financing would be a major problem because the substantial start-up costs would have to include banking for whatever loan guarantees the conduit would issue. Nor would the developing countries be likely supporters of the conduit because of the controls it would exercise over their financial affairs, including the requirement that all future government borrowing satisfy the conditions established by the conduit.

The concept of a secondary market for developing country loans is a good one, but we see no need for a conduit system. The framework for a secondary market has already emerged, interest among nonbanks is increasing, and a brokerage system is developing. Most important, the proper mechanism to facilitate transactions already exists in the form of transferable loan instruments. These developments, along with the trend toward the securitization of international lending, indicate that a secondary market will evolve on its own in response to market forces and without official stimulus.

Marking to Market. A mechanism for constraining both excessive borrowing and lending in the future has been proposed in the form of a requirement that the book value of foreign loans be periodically adjusted to reflect their value in the secondary market regardless of whether they are sold.[38] Under present accounting practices, banks carry their loans at book value as long as they hold them.

The mark-to-market proposal singles out foreign loans because of the presumed need to constrain excessive future foreign lending. However, the problem for the balance of the 1980s at least is not how to constrain excessive lending but how to prevent the already extremely low level of foreign lending from falling even lower. In the interest of the stability of the international financial system as well as consistency with the treatment of domestic loans, we believe the present book-value approach should be retained.

Cash-Flow Matching

Cash-flow matching is a process of easing the burden of debt service and reducing the risk of default by matching the time profile of repayment obligations to the profile of resources available for debt service. Perfect cash-flow matching is impossible to achieve. Nevertheless, improvements can be made over the present system of international commercial bank lending, where repayment terms are completely independent of the condition of the borrowing country's domestic economy and its earnings of foreign exchange.

The preponderence of floating interest rates in international commercial lending underlines the desirability of some degree of cash-flow matching. Inflation leads to higher interest rates, in effect accelerating amortization and making the terms of loans inconsistent with the gestation period of long-term development projects. Moreover, an increase in interest rates may coincide with a deterioration of the borrower's foreign exchange position. This juxtaposition of events occurred in 1981 and 1982, when both the prices and the volumes of Third World commodity exports collapsed. Repayment capacity shrank while repayment obligations increased because of the rise of interest rates.

Finance linked to capacity to pay may mean higher average costs by requiring that a risk premium be paid to lenders for this protection. However, the finance may be less costly in terms of the economic welfare of the borrowing country by limiting repayment obligations when the capacity to meet them is low.

Reimbursable Interest Averaging Cap. Under this proposal, a ceiling would be set by the lending bank on the interest rate (LIBOR or U.S. prime, plus spread) for the loan. If the market rate exceeds the ceiling, the excess due in interest payments would be deferred and capitalized. If the market rate subsequently declines below the ceiling, the borrower would continue to pay at the ceiling rate until all previously deferred funds are paid. At this point, the interest rate would return to the market rate. If the market rate remained above the ceiling, the interest deferred into principal would become reimbursable at maturity in a balloon payment or would be payable over an additional period.[39]

Band on Interest Rate Changes. This concept is very similar to the reimbursable interest averaging cap. The interest rate used to calculate payment during any given period would be constrained within a band (e.g., plus or minus half a percentage point) of the interest rate used to calculate the previous interest payment. Any change in the market interest rate exceeding the band would be reflected in an increase in the principal. As with the reimbursable cap, the borrower would be protected from sharp interest fluctuations and the lender would be protected from the adverse effect of interest forgiveness.[40]

Variable-Maturity Loan. This instrument has the same stabilization effect, but it varies the principal payment rather than the interest payment. A variable-maturity loan allows interest rates to change to reflect market conditions but limits the fluctuation in debt-service payments by allowing the size of the principal payment to vary with changes in interest rates. Thus, a rise in the interest rate results in a fall in amortization and hence an automatic extension in the maturity of the loan.[41]

One of the new cofinancing instruments adopted by the World Bank in 1983 functions in connection with variable-maturity loans. This instrument, known as *contingency liability financing,* allows private banks to make variable-maturity loans to a developing country with the World Bank agreeing to make a loan equal to the unamortized principal outstanding at the original maturity. Thus far, this arrangement has not been widely used.

The wider use of cash-flow matching instruments in commercial bank lending should be encouraged as a means of increasing the ability of borrowers to service debt in a timely manner. In addition, the multilateral development banks, particularly the World Bank, should promote the use of cash-flow matching by offering such options in their own lending to developing countries.

Compensatory Financing Facility for Interest Fluctuations. This proposal also seeks to mitigate the effects of interest rate increases on the balance-of-payments of developing countries. It would extend the IMF's Compensatory Financing Facility (CFF), which was created in 1963 to provide loans to members experiencing temporary export shortfalls due to external circumstances. For the developing countries, sharp interest rate increases can be as damaging and as uncontrollable as export shortfalls. A CFF for interest rates would address this problem.

The IMF could probably not bear the entire burden of lending necessitated by such a facility without an increase in its resources. Nevertheless, it might provide a portion of the financing (i.e., one-third to one-half) without calling for new capital. For example, the IMF could share the costs with the banks and the developing countries, with each party being responsible for one-third of the necessary financing. The CFF for interest fluctuations could be integrated with the IMF's existing compensatory facility so that the net foreign exchange position of the developing country would be taken into account in determining eligibility for CFF financing.

We recommend that serious consideration be given to ways of extending the CFF to cover interest rate fluctuations.

Insurance and Guarantees

Another means of decreasing the risks and increasing the flow of commercial bank lending to developing countries is the use of insurance and guarantees.

Existing Insurance Programs. Insurance programs already exist to a limited extent in international credit markets. Export credit agencies in all OECD countries have some type of insurance program. Because their main purpose is export promotion, the insurance is normally limited to credits for specific trade transactions. It is therefore of only limited usefulness in augmenting the flow of general development finance.

The World Bank has broad authority under its charter to guarantee private development lending to Third World countries, but in practice, the Bank uses its authority only in connection with cofinancing to guarantee the later maturities of commercial bank loans. Even in this context, however, guarantees are used sparingly because under the Bank's charter, a guarantee preempts its lending authority on a one-for-one basis. More extensive use of World Bank guarantees would require amendment of its charter (as we propose in Chapter 4) to reduce the impact of a guarantee on its ability to make loans directly.

Of the many issues to be considered in establishing an insurance program for commercial lending to developing countries, two stand out as particularly important: the form of the coverage and whether it should be through an official agency or the private market.

Form of Coverage. The main question is whether the insurance should be on individual loans or on the entire loan portfolios of banks. Insuring individual loans is subject to two major shortcomings: First, there is the moral hazard problem. Once lenders and borrowers have entered into insured loan contracts, the borrowers might more readily be tempted to engage in practices that increase the risk. Second, the insurance agency, by granting or denying guarantees for individual loans, would have a major role in the allocation of credit. The agency could avoid this problem by adjusting its premiums for individual loans on the basis of its evaluation of risks, but this would be both demanding in terms of resources and politically sensitive, particularly if the insurer were an official organization.[42]

A simpler and more effective form of coverage would be the insurance of a percentage of a bank's entire portfolio of loans to developing countries. The banks would retain control over the allocation of credit, and premiums would be based on the quality of the overall portfolio, not the riskiness of individual loans.

Assuming that insurance were to cover loan portfolios, the fraction of the portfolio to be covered would have to be determined. Based on the historical average of nonperforming loans for banks, Henry Wallich has concluded that insuring as little as 2 percent would provide a considerable margin of safety, although not total protection.[43] To encourage prudence in bank lending, he suggests that coverage of each individual loan in the portfolio be limited to some large percentage of its value.

Another question is whether the insurance should cover only transfer risk or should include commercial risk as well. What distinguishes lending abroad from lending at home is not the normal commercial risk but the risk of default induced by the borrower's inability to obtain foreign exchange to service the loan. The main need, therefore, is for insuring banks against transfer risk. Moreover, the normal credit risk of most bank loans to developing countries is guaranteed by the countries' governments. Limiting the insurance to the type of risk that is is external to a borrowing firm also would align the insurance more closely with OPIC and MIGA insurance programs for foreign direct investment in which so-called political risks, but not commercial risks, are covered.

Official versus Private. Insurance of bank portfolios could be accomplished through either official or private facilities. If an official agency were contemplated, it could be established at the national or international level. Although any insurance facility should be self-sustaining over the long run, it would need public funds initially until it had time to accumulate adequate reserves. So long as the debt crisis continues, however, public support for such official financing would probably be lacking. Even if the insurance were limited to new loans, official financing would undoubtedly be regarded as a bailout of the banks.

In principle, the insurance of bank portfolios against transfer risk could be accomplished through the existing private insurance market. Private insurance has increasingly been covering a variety of loan obligations, including trade credits, municipal bond issues, and corporate debt. As a practical matter, however, the extension of private insurance into this area may not be an easy step until further progress is made in resolving the debt crisis. In this context, the collapse of the Citibank-CIGNA agreement is significant. In late 1984, Citibank arranged with CIGNA to provide $900 million in transfer risk insurance on a portfolio of loans to heavily indebted developing countries. The agreement carried an annual premium of half of one percent of principal, a rate regarded in banking and insurance circles as exceptionally low for transfer risk insurance.[44] It also included a $50-million deductible for each country covered. However, CIGNA was unable to obtain the expected participation of other insurance companies and subsequently terminated the agreement at the expense of a cancellation fee.

The failure of the agreement was in large part due to its coverage of existing loans to countries experiencing serious debt-servicing difficulties and the concern that the problem was being passed on to the insurance industry. Restriction of insurance to portfolios of new obligations of countries showing solid progress in overcoming the debt problem would improve the prospects for an active insurance market for loans to developing countries. The potential pool of insurance for such purposes has been estimated at $10 billion.

Insurance for New Loans. We believe that the establishment of a private insurance market to cover the transfer risk on new loans to Third World countries would be a healthy development. By spreading the risks to additional participants in the intermediation process, it would reduce the vulnerability of the lending institutions while helping to increase and stabilize the flow of external capital to developing countries.

Mainly for moral hazard reasons, we favor a form of coverage in which a modest percentage of a bank's entire portfolio of loans to developing countries would be insured, with coverage of each individual loan limited to some large percentage of its value.

Role of Multilateral Financial Institutions

The roles of the IMF and the World Bank in relation to commercial lending are likely to be strengthened in the coming years by the plan proposed by U.S. Treasury Secretary Baker at the October 1985 meetings of the two institutions in Seoul. Although the Baker initiative was triggered by the continuing severe debt problems of many developing countries, it inevitably will have a longer-run impact on the part played by the multilateral financial institutions in linking external flows of capital to fundamental policy reforms in the highly indebted countries.

The Baker initiative implies a more active concern by the U.S. government about developments in the Third World in the aftermath of the debt crisis. Fundamentally, it recognizes that more is needed than austerity measures if the debtor countries are to achieve not only short-run balance-of-payments adjustment but also sustainable long-run growth. The initiative's three elements apply, respectively, to the highly indebted countries, the multilateral financial institutions, and the commercial banks.

First, the initiative calls for comprehensive structural reforms in the indebted developing countries to promote sustained growth in addition to macroeconomic policies to reduce inflation and improve the balance-of-payments. Heretofore, proposals for overcoming the debt crisis were concentrated on demand-reducing measures in the areas of fiscal, monetary, and exchange rate policy. These measures have brought substantial improvements in payments' balances, but at the cost of declines in the growth of output, rising unemployment, and falling per capita income in many indebted countries.

The initiative emphasizes the need for parallel "supply-side actions to mobilize domestic savings and facilitate efficient investment, both domestic and foreign, by means of tax reform, labor market reform and the development of financial markets." It also calls for increased reliance on the private sector and greater emphasis on "market-opening measures to encourage foreign direct investment and capital inflows, as well as to liberalize trade."[45]

The second element stresses the important role of the multilateral financial institutions in encouraging the needed policy reforms in conjunction with their lending programs and in catalyzing an increased flow of private financing. The plan calls upon the World Bank and the Interamerican Development Bank (IDB) to step up disbursements to the principal debtors to an average of $9 billion annually during the 1986–1988 period, an increase of 50 percent from the current level of about $6 billion.

We endorse in particular the expansion of the World Bank's fast-disbursing structural and sectoral adjustment lending in support of growth-oriented policies and institutional and sectoral reform. Such program lending is generally a more effective vehicle for influencing domestic policies in the developing countries than the traditional World Bank lending tied to individual projects.

The third element calls on the commercial banking community to make a corresponding commitment to help support the principal debtor countries to make the transition to stronger growth. It requests net new lending from the commercial banks in the range of $20 billion over the 1986–1988 period.

Such a commitment by the commercial banks will require firm assurances that the debtor countries are prepared to take the necessary reform measures that will lead to healthy economic growth and improved debt ratios. Central to the entire strategy is much closer cooperation between the World Bank and the IMF than in the past in coordinating their lending and policy advice. The commercial banks will look to these institutions to certify on a case-by-case basis whether individual debtor countries have met the standards that will qualify them for additional loans.

The Baker plan is a laudable American initiative. Nevertheless, we should not lose sight of the international character of lending to the Third World. Other industrial countries and their banks have collectively a far greater stake in the resolution of the debt problem than their U.S. counterparts. The exposure of the non-U.S. banks in the major debtor countries is almost twice that of the U.S. banks, and the exposure of the other industrial countries in the World Bank is twice that of the United States.[46] These statistics underline the importance of the multilateral financial institutions, rather than the United States, assuming the crucial role in the management of international creditor-debtor relations over the long run.

Institute of International Finance

Overlending by the commercial banks in the 1970s and early 1980s was due in part to the inadequacy of the information available to them to assess the creditworthiness of developing country borrowers. To remedy this deficiency, the Institute of International Finance (IIF) was established early in 1983 as a private nonprofit organization with a membership consisting of lending institutions from all parts of the world.

The IIF's principal purpose is to improve the timeliness and quality of information on borrowing countries. It provides its members with statistical information on forty developing countries, including data on the domestic economy, trade, balance of payments, monetary aggregates, and longer-term structural change. It also prepares reports on individual countries based on staff visits. These reports contain a review of the country's economic situation and policies, balance-of-payments prospects, and financing requirements. In addition, the IIF provides information on trends in international lending, the state of rescheduling arrangements with banks and official creditors, and the structure of debt.

Beyond its information function, the IIF encourages communication among the major participants in the lending process, including banks, borrowing countries, multilateral organizations (especially the IMF and World Bank), and government regulatory bodies. It also sponsors study groups on issues of long-term concern to lenders such as insurance and guarantees, regulation, accounting, and tax treatment of cross-border lending.

One thing the institute does *not* do is provide credit ratings of individual borrowing countries. Such ratings by a collective instrumentality of the banks might well have adverse antitrust implications. Moreover, a low credit rating could be self-fulfilling by inducing a cutoff of new lending. In any case, it is wise to let each bank form its own judgment about the creditworthiness of borrowers on the basis of all the information at its disposal, including that provided by the IIF. Given the confidentiality of much of the data transmitted by borrowing countries to the IMF and the World Bank, the IIF fulfills an important function in enabling banks to make sounder judgments about the risks involved in lending to developing countries.

International Bond Markets

With the falloff in commercial bank lending to developing countries in recent years, what are the prospects for mobilizing private loan capital through the international securities markets?

In a sense, the developing countries continue to have indirect access to the bond markets through the multilateral development banks. The World Bank and the regional development banks are major borrowers in those markets and onlend the proceeds to their developing country members.

However, direct borrowing in the international securities markets has played only a modest role for developing countries compared with that of commercial bank lending. Relatively few developing countries have succeeded in issuing international bonds, and then only for small amounts.[47]

Trends in Bond Issues

In the 1960s and early 1970s, international bond issues by the developing countries rarely exceeded $100 million and averaged little more than 3 percent of total issues. By 1978, however, developing countries had increased their borrowing to $5.2 billion and their share of total international bond issues to 15 percent (see Table 24). The peak year for Third World bond issues was 1978. The volume declined sharply in 1979 and 1980 because of the increase in the availability of bank lending and the contraction of fixed-rate bonds in the face of the uncertainties of inflation and interest rates. Although there was some recovery in the volume of Third World bond issues beginning in 1981, their market share has fallen to the lowest point in ten years.

Despite the recovery in the volume of issues in the early 1980s, the number of developing countries able to resort to the international bond market has been declining in recent years. In 1978, twenty-five emerging countries successfully floated international bond issues. This number remained fairly stable until the debt crisis restricted access to all but the most creditworthy countries. By 1983, the number of developing countries issuing bonds in international markets had fallen by one-third; and 80 percent of the volume was accounted for by only five countries.[48]

The debt crisis also led to a change in the composition of borrowers. Until 1982, Mexico, Brazil, and Venezuela were generally among the major issuers. Since late 1982, none of them has issued a bond in the

Table 24

International Bond Issues and Placements, 1965, 1970, and 1975 to 1984
(billions of dollars)

Type of Issue or Placement	1965	1970	1975	1976	1977	1978	1979	1980	1981	1982	1983	1984
Issues or placements in foreign markets	2.4	2.4	12.3	18.9	16.6	20.7	20.3	17.9	20.5	25.0	27.1	27.8
Amount by developing countries	0.1	0.1	0.5	0.9	1.6	2.2	1.2	0.6	1.1	0.6	0.6	1.2
Percent by developing countries	4.2	4.2	4.1	4.8	9.6	10.6	5.9	3.4	5.4	2.4	2.2	4.3
Issues in the Eurobond market	0.9	3.5	10.5	15.4	19.5	14.9	18.6	20.4	31.3	50.3	50.1	81.7
Amount by developing countries	0.0	0.1	0.2	1.1	2.5	3.0	1.9	1.2	3.1	3.7	2.1	2.6
Percent by developing countries	0.0	2.9	1.9	7.1	12.8	20.1	10.2	5.9	9.9	7.4	4.2	3.2
Total international bond issues	3.3	5.9	22.8	34.3	36.1	35.6	33.9	38.3	51.8	75.5	77.2	109.5
Amount by developing countries	0.1	0.2	0.7	2.0	4.1	5.2	3.1	1.8	4.2	4.3	2.7	3.8
Percent by developing countries	3.0	3.4	3.1	5.8	11.4	14.6	8.0	4.7	8.1	5.7	3.5	3.5
Issues of floating-rate notes												
Amount by all entities	-	-	0.3	1.4	2.2	2.9	4.2	4.8	11.3	15.3	19.5	38.2
Percent of total bond issues	-	-	1.3	4.1	6.1	8.1	10.8	12.5	21.8	20.3	25.2	34.9

Note: Details may not add to totals because of rounding.
Source: World Bank, World Development Report 1985, p. 122. Based on: OECD Financial Statistics 1971, OECD Financial Market Trends 1984.

international market; all the major borrowers have been East Asian countries (Indonesia, Korea, Malaysia, and Thailand).

The recent exclusion of the major debtors from the international bond market reflects the difference in the relationship with the borrowing country between bondholders on the one hand and the banks on the other. Unlike the banks, bondholders have only a remote relationship with the borrowing country. In case of debt-service difficulties, the risk of loss to the bondholders through outright default has been perceived by the market as greater than that to which the banks are exposed from a rescheduling. Moreover, the banks have been encouraged to continue to lend by an implicit assumption that national financial authorities would assist them in coping with a systemic debt crisis in developing countries.

Despite the market's perception of greater risk to bondholders than to bank lenders,[49] most developing countries have continued to meet the interest and principal payments on their outstanding bonds and have excluded bond payments from reschedulings. The continued servicing of bonded debt has had a strongly favorable effect on the differential between the yields on developing country bonds and those on industrial country bonds in the secondary markets. For example, the yield differential on Brazilian bonds rose from about 2 percent in the first half of 1982 to as much as 6 percent during certain periods of 1983. However, by late 1983 and early 1984, the differential had declined to approximately 3 percent. Narrowing spreads were also experienced by Mexican and Venezuelan bonds. This trend in yield differentials implies a substantial improvement in the market's perception of the risk in holding bonds of developing countries.

Floating-Rate Notes

The substantial growth of the international bond market in the 1980s has been stimulated by the creation of floating-rate notes (see Table 24). These are medium-term securities carrying a variable interest rate. Generally, the rate is set for three and six months and is a fixed margin over the prevailing LIBOR rate for Eurodollar deposits. Floating-rate notes were first issued in the Eurobond market in 1970. The growth in the volume of such notes was slow during the 1970s but has increased rapidly in the past few years. In 1984, floating-rate notes accounted for 35 percent of all international bond issues.

Only a few developing countries have managed to break into this market. Mexico and Brazil had issued floating-rate notes before their debt difficulties in 1982. Since then, a few East Asian countries have entered the market. These countries account for the bulk of all bonds issued by developing countries in the past few years, and floating-rate notes make up nearly one-half of the total. For Thailand and Malaysia, floating-rate notes have provided financing below the cost of syndicated loans.

Because most floating-rate notes are bought by the commercial banks, they do not provide the means for developing countries to diversify their creditors. Moreover, they require the borrowers to bear the interest rate risk. Nevertheless, developing countries should be encouraged to seek access to this market as their creditworthiness improves. Because floating-rate notes are more marketable than fixed-rate securities, they may provide the basis for some developing countries to gain later access to the fixed-rate market. At the same time, these notes may prove to be a less expensive source of external finance than syndicated loans.

Outlook

The debt crisis ended the developing countries' easy access to private international financing. Commercial lending to the developing countries is unlikely to return to the excessive levels of the late 1970s and early 1980s.

Prospects for the expansion of commercial lending beyond today's depressed levels will depend mainly on three sets of factors: less expansionary macroeconomic policies and more rational systems of economic incentives in developing countries, encouraged and supported by the World Bank, the IMF, and other multilateral financial institutions; an improved world economic environment sustained by a better mix of fiscal and monetary policies in the United States and other industrial countries; and improvements and innovations in the mechanisms for private lending to foreign borrowers, both through the commercial banks and the rapidly growing international securities markets.

However, no changes in commercial lending practices can substitute for the needed reforms in the public policies of the developing countries. As sound policies are put in place, the creditworthiness of the developing countries will be gradually restored, and an improved commercial lending system will become a more effective vehicle for contributing to world economic development.

Notes

Chapter 1

1. GATT, *International Trade, 1982–83* (Geneva, 1983), Table A17.

2. IMF, *International Capital Markets* (Washington, D.C., July 1983), Table 1.

3. GATT, *International Trade, 1984–85,* Table A34, and U.S. Department of Commerce, *Survey of Current Business,* August 1984, p. 22.

4. Morgan Guaranty Trust Company, *World Financial Markets,* March/April 1985, Table 3.

5. OECD, *Development Cooperation, 1984 Review* (Paris, 1984), Table II.A.1. The figure refers to flows from DAC countries, which include the United States, Canada, Japan, Australia, New Zealand, and the Western European countries.

6. The World Bank defines *middle-income* countries as those with a 1984 GNP per capita of $400 or more. Within that group, countries such as Korea, Malaysia, Brazil, and Mexico, with incomes above $1,635 per capita, are designated as *upper middle income.*

7. *World Bank World Development Report, 1987.* The theme of this report is that developing countries that pursue more open trading policies are likely to have better success in industrialization and in their overall economic performance.

Chapter 2

1. W. Arthur Lewis, *The Theory of Economic Growth* (Homewood, Ill.: Richard D. Irwin, 1955), p. 226.

2. World Bank, *World Development Report 1985,* Annex Table 5. *Investment and savings ratios* refers to gross domestic investment and gross domestic savings, respectively, as a percent of gross domestic product.

3. World Bank, *World Development Report 1983,* p. 37.

4. World Bank, *World Development Report 1983,* p. 43.

5. IMF, *World Economic Outlook,* April 1986, p. 58.

6. IMF, *World Economic Outlook,* September 1984, Appendix Table 17.

7. Mohsin S. Khan and Malcolm Knight, "Sources of Payments Problems in LDCs," *Finance and Development,* December 1983, p. 4.

8. IMF, *World Economic Outlook,* April 1986, Appendix Table 40. The table shows the excess of current-account financing as "errors and omissions," which reached a peak of $26.3 billion in 1982.

9. Morgan Guaranty Trust Company of New York, *World Financial Markets,* October/November 1984, p. 3. See also John T. Cuddington, "Capital Flight: Estimates, Issues and Explanations," *Princeton Studies in International Finance,* forthcoming.

10. Rudiger Dormbusch, "External Debt, Budget Deficits, and Disequilibrium Exchange Rates," National Bureau of Economic Research Working Paper No. 1336.

11. Separating the two markets would involve some government controls. But the burden of administration would be less than under a system of comprehensive controls. For a fuller discussion, see Henry Wallich and Thomas C. Glaessner, "Financial Regulation in the United States and in Developing Countries," Federal Reserve Board, 26 February 1985.

12. Recent empirical studies by two IMF staff members show that countries with higher shares of public investment in total investment tend to have lower growth rates. Mario I. Blejer and Mohsin S. Khan, "Private Investment in Developing Countries," *Finance and Development,* June 1984.

13. World Bank, *Toward Sustained Development in Sub-Saharan Africa,* 1984, p. 24.

14. World Bank, *World Development Report 1984,* Appendix Table 21.

15. OECD, *Development Cooperation: 1983 Review,* Paris, 1983, p. 25.

16. World Bank, *World Development Report 1983,* pp. 60–61.

Chapter 3

1. World Bank, *Towards Sustained Development in Sub-Saharan Africa,* 1984, p. 17.

2. James Riedel, *Myth and Reality of External Constraints on Development,* Thames Essay Series (Trade Policy Research Centre) 1987.

3. Riedel, *Myth and Reality of External Constraints on Development.* The quote is from John Adler, "The World Bank's Concept of Development," in J.N. Bhagwati and R. Eakans, eds., *Foreign Aid,* (Penguin), p. 36.

4. See, for example, John Williamson and Donald Lessard, op. cit., pp. 20 ff.

5. Henry C. Wallich, Comments on "Perspective on the External Debt Situation" (comments presented at the annual meeting of the American Economic Association, December 28, 1984), p. 3.

6. OECD, *Development Cooperation: 1984 Review* (Paris, 1984), p. 66.

7. World Bank, *World Development Report 1984,* Chapter 3.

8. World Bank, *World Development Report 1984,* p. 35. Actually, the "High Case" scenario shows capital flows to the developing countries in 1995 at a level $30 billion higher than in the "Low Case" but with a ratio of debt service to exports lower than that of the "Low Case" (p. 38).

9. Twenty-six Economists, *Promoting World Recovery: A Statement on Global Economic Strategy* (Washington, D.C.: Institute for International Economics, December 1982).

10. Morgan Guaranty Trust Company, *World Financial Markets,* statistical appendix, various issues.

11. Morgan Guaranty Trust Company, *World Financial Markets.*

12. Henry Wallich, "The U.S. Budget Deficit and Its International Repercussions" (Remarks to the List Gesellschaft, Frankfurt, West Germany, April 6, 1984).

13. GATT, *Trade Policies for a Better Future: Proposals for Action* (Geneva, March 1985). Also known as the report of the "Wise Men."

Chapter 4

1. OECD, *Twenty-Five Years of Development Cooperation: 1985 Report,* p. 127.

2. This definition of official development assistance has been established by the DAC of the OECD, and its usage has been generally adopted. Excluded from such assistance are military assistance and any loans with maturities of less than one year.

3. The grant element is calculated as the difference between the face value of the loan and the present value of the stream of repayments discounted at the market rate. Thus, the grant element of a grant is 100 percent, whereas that of a loan at the market rate is zero. The grant equivalent of a concessional loan can fall anywhere between those extremes.

4. Because of debt rescheduling, it is necessary to incorporate short-term bank lending into bank sector flows in order to get a meaningful picture of total private flows since 1981. As shown in Table 10, short-term bank lending fell sharply after 1981 and turned negative in 1983 as a large volume of such loans were rescheduled for longer terms.

5. OECD, *Twenty-Five Years of Development Cooperation: 1985 Report,* p. 319.

6. Foreign Assistance and Related Programs Appropriations Bill, 1979, S. R. 1194, 95:2 (1978) p. 79.

7. OECD, *Twenty-five Years of Development Cooperation, 1985 Report,* p. 309.

8. OECD, *Development Cooperation: 1984 Review,* Table II.G.3, pp. 230, 233.

9. U.S. Agency for International Development, *Approaches to the Policy Dialogue,* December 1982, p. 6.

10. John Sewell and Christine Contee, "U.S. Foreign Aid in the 1980s: Reordering Priorities," Chapter 4 in *U.S. Foreign Policy and the Third World: Agenda 1985–86,* Overseas Development Council, 1985, p. 108.

11. OECD, *Twenty-Five Years of Development Cooperation: 1985 Report,* p. 331.

12. Keizai Doyukai, *Toward Active Participation in the Management of Global Affairs* (Tokyo, April 1984).

13. Expanded Japanese development assistance would also help to rectify the severe imbalance in world trade, especially if the assistance were provided on an untied basis.

14. Robert L. Ayres, "Concessional Resources and Prospects for the Low-Income Countries" (paper prepared for December 1983 meetings of the American Economic Association), p. 8.

15. The Commission on Security and Economic Assistance, *A Report to the Secretary of State,* November 1983, p. 47. The commission was chaired by Frank C. Carlucci, president of Sears World Trade, Inc., and included members of Congress and representatives of business, labor, and the private nonprofit sector.

16. OECD, *Development Cooperation, 1983 Review,* Table D.4, p. 198.

17. *Associated financing* consists mainly of mixed credits but also includes credits combining official development assistance with nonconcessional flows other than export credits. See OECD, *Development Cooperation: 1984 Review,* Chapter VIII.

18. In late October 1984, the Export-Import Bank and AID collaborated on the first U.S. mixed-credit package to help a U.S. firm compete for a $25-million sale of locomotives to Botswana. Although it included an AID grant of $4.5 million, the terms were still not favorable enough to win the sale against mixed-credit competition from Canada.

19. In June 1983, the OECD adopted the "DAC Guiding Principles or the Use of Aid in Association with Export Credits and Other Market Funds." Among the objectives of the principles is the strengthening of transparency and discipline in the area of mixed credits, but the success of the effort is as yet unclear.

20. During the 1980–1982 period, only 40 percent of DAC official development assistance (and an even lesser percentage of U.S. official development assistance was allocated to low-income countries as defined by the World Bank (per capita income less than $400). In contrast, two-thirds of multilateral concessional assistance flowed to these countries.

21. U.S. Treasury, *United States Participation in the Multilateral Development Banks in the 1980s* (Washington, D.C., 1982), p. 157.

22. U.S. Department of State, "Multilateral Development Banks," *GIST,* November 1984.

23. Actual U.S. appropriations have fallen behind this schedule.

24. IDA loans have carried the following terms: fifty-year maturities; grace periods of ten years during which no amortization is required; no interest charge; a commitment fee of 0.50 percent on the undisbursed balance; and a service charge of 0.75 percent on the disbursed amount. However, as recommended by the IDA Deputies on September 25, 1986, these loans in the future should carry thirty-five- to forty-year maturities.

25. World Bank, *IDA in Retrospect* (Washington, D.C., 1982), p. 23.

26. For example, the UNDP review in the early 1980s revealed that there were approximately 600 projects on the books from sixty donors in Kenya and 614 from sixty-nine donors in Zambia. World Bank, *World Development Report 1985,* p. 107.

27. IMF, *Annual Report 1975,* p. 88.

28. Richard Goode, *Economic Assistance to the Developing Countries: An Enlarged Role for the International Monetary Fund,* Brookings Discussion Papers in International Economics, November 1984, p. 39.

29. The overlap of the two institutions is further illustrated by the establishment by the IMF in March 1986 of a new Structural Adjustment Facility (SAF). This facility will make loans on concessional terms to low-income countries that

develop a medium-term policy framework. The framework would be developed jointly with the staff of both the IMF and the World Bank.

30. Ernest Stern, "World Bank Financing of Structural Adjustment Lending," in John Williamson, editor, *IMF Conditionality* (Institute for International Economics, 1983), p. 100.

31. Lester B. Pearson, Chairman, *Partners in Development,* Report of the Commission on International Development (Praeger, 1969), p. 230.

32. A. W. Clausen, "Promoting the Private Sector in Developing Countries" (Speech to the Institute of Directors, London, 26 February 1985).

33. World Bank, *Cofinancing,* 1983.

34. A similar organization on a regional basis was established in September 1985 to serve a catalytic role in mobilizing domestic and foreign private capital for Latin America. Named the Inter-American Investment Corporation; it is affiliated with the Inter-American Development Bank and is capitalized at $200 million.

Chapter 5

1. Statement of Secretary James Baker before the Joint Annual Meeting of the IMF and World Bank, Seoul, Korea, 8 October 1985.

2. Nicholas D. Kristof, "Curbs Give Way to Welcome for Multinational Companies," *New York Times,* 11 May 1985.

3. Although the total returns on direct investment are correlated with a country's ability to service those payments, there is evidence that the portion remitted as dividends to the parent firm tends to be less affected by short-term variations in profits. Most of the swings are absorbed by the substantial share of earnings that is reinvested. IMF, *Foreign Investment in Developing Countries,* Occasional Paper 33, January 1985, p. 23.

4. According to UNCTAD, 13 percent of outstanding loans by the ten largest U.S. banks to Latin American countries in 1982 went to transnational corporation subsidaries in those countries. UNCTAD, "The Role of Foreign Direct Investment in Development Finance: Current Issues," TD/B/C.3/196, Geneva, 14 December 1984.

5. For three reasons, the official data on direct investment tend to understate the importance of this form of resource transfer to developing countries. First, the data do not normally include the value of nonfinancial resources, such as technology and management, that usually accompany the financial flows. Second, foreign borrowing by the affiliate from sources other than the parent company is not counted as direct investment even when guaranteed by the parent. And third, new forms of participation in foreign enterprises by multinational corporations, such as management contracts and production-sharing arrangements, do not get reflected in the data when the percentage of equity and other long-term capital in the foreign venture falls below the minimum qualifying for treatment as direct investment.

6. IMF, *Foreign Investment in Developing Countries,* p. 3.

7. U.S. Department of Commerce, *International Direct Investment* (August 1984), p. 47, Tables 4 and 5.

8. OECD, *Investing in Developing Countries* (Paris, 1983), pp. 19–20.

9. IMF, *Foreign Investment in Developing Countries,* p. 43, Table A.4.

10. IMF, *Foreign Investment in Developing Countries,* p. 7. Income receipts include reinvested earnings. In present balance-of-payments accounting, reinvested earnings enter twice: once as an income receipt in the current account and once as an outflow of direct investment in the capital account.

11. The data on both outflows and inflows include reinvested earnings. U.S. Department of Commerce, *International Direct Investment* (August 1984) Appendix Tables 9 and 13.

12. Unfortunately, the World Bank commits a similar error in using the concept of *net transfers* in its analysis of the debt problem of developing countries. *Net transfers* is the difference between net lending to a country in a given year and interest paid by the country during the same year on its outstanding debt. When a country's interest payments exceed its receipts of new loans (less amortization), it is deemed to be suffering a negative net transfer. Applying that concept to the example of U.S. direct investment in the developing countries in 1980 and 1981, those countries would be regarded as experiencing a negative resource transfer averaging $6 billion a year, with all the adverse connotations of that expression.

13. Robert E. Lipsey and Irving B. Kravis, *U.S.-Owned Affiliates and Host-Country Exports,* Working Paper No. 1037, National Bureau of Economic Research, December 1982.

14. In assessing the effects of foreign investment, corrections can, in principle, be made for these types of distortions by the use of *shadow prices* that correspond more closely than actual prices to the real costs of inputs to society and the real benefits of outputs.

15. Robert E. Lipsey and Merle Yahr Weiss, "Foreign Production and Exports of Individual Firms," *Review of Economic and Statistics,* May 1984.

16. For a fuller discussion of this issue, see the policy statement, *Work and Change: Labor Market Adjustments in a Competitive World* (New York: Committee for Economic Development, 1987).

17. A more comprehensive treatment of host- and home-country policies toward foreign direct investment is contained in: Isaiah Frank, *Foreign Enterprise in Developing Countries,* a Supplementary Paper of the Committee for Economic Development; (Baltimore, MD: The Johns Hopkins University Press, 1980), and the policy statement *Transnational Corporations and Developing Countries: New Policies for a Changing World Economy* (New York: Committee for Economic Development, April 1981).

18. A good example is the recent agreement reached between IBM and the Mexican government. Under its terms, IBM is allowed to own 100 percent of the Mexican subsidiary that will manufacture personal computers. But IBM is required to export 90 percent of the computers it makes in Mexico. In addition, the company agreed to set up a semiconductor development center for local industry, purchase a variety of high-technology components from Mexican sources,

and produce softwear in Mexico for the Latin American market. "IBM Concessions to Mexico," *The New York Times,* 25 July 1985.

19. See, for example, Labor-Industry Coalition for International Trade, *Performance Requirements* Washington, D.C., May 1981).

20. The provision applies only to products from new facilities established by American firms after the date of enactment of the 1984 law. This grandfather clause was adopted to accommodate U.S. automotive manufacturers that have large foreign investments subject to performance requirements. Thus far, the provision has not been activated, and no guidelines have been issued for its application.

21. "Foreign Investments in the Brazilian Economy," *Brazil Trade and Industry,* December 1984.

22. White House, *Statement by the President* and *International Investment Policy Statement,* Washington, D.C., 9 September 1983.

23. The annual limits on these authorities are $15 million for direct loans and $150 million for general credit guarantees.

24. Ibrahim F. I. Shihata, "Increasing Private Capital Flows to LDCs," *Finance and Development,* December 1984, pp. 7–8.

25. The predecessors to these treaties are the bilateral commercial treaties between the United States and other countries that had been entered into since the earliest days of the Republic. They are generically known as Treaties of Friendship, Commerce and Navigation, and over forty are currently in force, half of them negotiated after World War II. Because of their complex content, efforts to extend them to developing countries produced limited results, and the program was effectively phased out by the mid-1960s.

26. More limited undertakings are contained in bilateral agreements between OPIC and governments of host countries as a condition for OPIC insurance of investments in those countries. However, these agreements do not include standards for the treatment of foreign investors but are concerned entirely with the obligations of the host country to the U.S. government as subrogator to the claims of the investor. The bilateral OPIC agreements therefore cannot serve as models for more limited forms of bilateral investment treaties.

27. A survey of the views of multinationals on host-country policies found that with few exceptions, the Calvo doctrine "was not regarded as a significant deterrent to private foreign direct investment in developing countries." See Frank, *Foreign Investment in Developing Countries,* p. 106.

28. See, for example, Charles P. Kindleberger, "U.S. Policy Toward Direct Investment with Special Reference to the Less Developed Countries," in *United States International Economic Policy in an Interdependent World* (Washington, D.C., July 1971).

29. Occasionally, conflicts of jurisdiction arise between host- and home-country legislation. In such cases, host-country laws generally take precedence.

30. In addition to the public programs, Lloyd's of London pioneered a private political risk insurance market for foreign investments and export contracts. By 1982, the aggregate liability under private policies was around $8 billion.

31. It is precisely fear of excessive influence and leverage over domestic policies that has led a number of key developing countries to express reservations about MIGA.

32. The reasons are historically rooted differences in copyright principles between U.S. law and the Berne Convention established in 1886. Among these differences have been the U.S. requirement for certain formalities (e.g., notice of copyright) and for domestic printing of English-language works of U.S. authors.

33. Jacques J. Gorlin, "Copyright Protection for Computer Software and the Next Round of Multilateral Trade Negotiations," 1 June 1985, p. 47.

34. *Wall Street Journal,* April 8, 1986.

35. Gorlin, "Copyright Protection for Computer Software and the Next Round of Multilateral Trade Negotiations," p. iii.

36. Donald Lessard and John Williamson, *Financial Intermediation Beyond the Debt Crisis* (Washington, D.C.: Institute of International Economics, September 1985) pp. 50–51.

37. Antoine W. van Agtmael, *Emerging Security Markets - Investment Banking Opportunities in the Developing World* (London: Euromoney Publications, 1984), p. 39.

38. "Agency Proposes Fund of Stocks in Third World," *New York Times,* 20 December 1985, p. D-5.

Chapter 6

1. World Bank, *World Debt Tables, 1985–86 Edition,* p. xi. Of this total, three-quarters is debt of original maturity of more than one year.

2. During the 1970–1982 period, the GDP of the middle-income developing countries (the principal borrowers from commercial banks) grew at an average annual rate of 5.4 percent compared with only 2.8 percent for the industrial countries. World Bank, *World Development Report 1984,* Annex Table 2.

3. IMF, *Recent Multilateral Debt Restructurings with Official and Bank Creditors,* Occasional Paper 25, December 1983, p. 1.

4. OECD, *External Debt of Developing Countries: 1983 Survey* (Paris, 1984), p. 16.

5. OECD, *External Debt of Developing Countries: 1983 Survey,* Table C, p. 27, and World Bank, *World Development Report 1985,* Table 2.1., p. 17.

6. IMF, *World Economic Outlook,* April 1985, p. 190.

7. W. Arthur Lewis, *The Evolution of the International Economic Order* (Princeton: Princeton University Press, 1978), p. 65.

8. IMF, *World Economic Outlook,* April 1985, Table 39, p. 252.

9. The more rapid rise of exports than GNP applies to developing countries as a whole and also to the middle-income group. It does not hold, however, for low-income African countries, where the share of exports in GNP fell steeply. These countries were particularly hard hit by the 1981–1982 world recession, which caused a reduction in both the prices and the volume of exports of primary materials. Although the economic recovery since 1983 brought some improvement in African exports, their terms of trade in 1983 were still below those of 1980.

10. The debt-service ratio is the ratio of interest payments plus amortization to exports.

11. IMF, *World Economic Outlook,* April 1986, p. 91.

12. In 1984 the combined current-account deficit of all developing countries was $44 billion. The deficit was $9 billion for those countries that obtained at least two-thirds of their external borrowing in 1978–1982 from commercial creditors. IMF, *World Economic Outlook,* April 1985, Table 29, p. 236.

13. In 1982, the debt-to-GNP ratios were 28.3 percent for Korea and 33.1 percent for Mexico. World Bank, *World Debt Tables, 1985–86 Edition,* pp. 217 and 329.

14. A comparison of Mexico and Korea may also reflect the greater difficulty of successful industrialization and export growth for basic commodity-exporting countries than for countries that were never highly dependent on primary commodities in the first place. Because the latter have generally pursued more diversified export strategies, they have had a more stable flow of foreign exchange and a greater capacity to withstand external economic shocks.

15. Common examples are state-owned steel mills and national-flag airlines that are regarded in may developing countries as symbols of power and development.

16. Mexico's experience is illustrative. In 1981–1982, its budget deficit more than doubled as a proportion of GNP and was financed partly by borrowing abroad. This sowed the seeds of its debt crisis in 1982.

17. William R. Cline, *International Debt: Systemic Risk and Policy Response* (Washington, D.C.: Institute for International Economics, 1984), p. 10; and World Bank, *World Debt Tables, 1984–85 Edition,* p. xi.

18. One way for the United States to strengthen its oil security while providing one-time assistance to Mexico would be to complete the authorized build-up of U.S. strategic petroleum reserves by purchase of Mexican oil. At present, the U.S. oil reserves are 250 million barrels short of the goal set in the 1970s. Mexico, by pumping one-half million barrels of oil a day for sale to the U.S. strategic reserve, would earn approximately $3 billion in a year, substantially reducing its loss due to the drop in price.

19. IMF, *World Economic Outlook,* 1984, p. 1.

20. Cline, *International Debt,* pp. 12–13.

21. World Bank, *World Development Report 1985,* p. 55.

22. For a fuller discussion of the relation between the U.S. budget deficit, international competitiveness and protection, see *Toll of The Twin Deficits* (CED: New York, 1987).

23. World Bank, *World Development Report 1985,* pp. 111–112.

24. IMF, *Recent Multilateral Debt Restructurings with Official and Bank Creditors,* Occasional Paper 25, December 1983. p. 7.

25. Commercial bank exposure to countries already in the process of restructuring their debt increased by 25 percent a year in the five years to 1981. IMF, *Recent Multilateral Debt Restructurings with Official and Bank Creditors.* p. 5.

26. Jack M. Guttentag and Richard J. Herring, *Disaster Myopia in International Banking,* Brookings Discussion Papers in International Economics No. 31, June

1985, p. 16. This section has benefited from this and other works by the same authors in the Brookings series.

27. David Folkerts-Landau, "The Changing Role of International Bank Lending in Development Finance," *IMF Staff Papers,* Vol. 32, No.2, June 1985, pp. 332 and 334.

28. Guttentag and Herring, *Disaster Myopia in International Banking,* p. 9.

29. In December 1983, five countries were reportedly placed in this category (Bolivia, Nicaragua, Poland, Sudan, and Zaire) with reserves set at 10 percent to 75 percent of the face value of loans. C. F. Bergsten, W. R. Cline, and John Williamson, *Bank Lending to Developing Countries: The Policy Alternatives* (Washington, D.C.: Institute for International Economics, April 1985), p. 29.

30. Guttentag and Herring, *The Current Crisis in International Lending,* p. 25.

31. "Revisions to Guidelines for Capital Adequacy," *Federal Reserve Bulletin,* Washington, D.C., June 1985, p. 440.

32. Jack M. Guttentag and Richard J. Herring, *Disaster Myopia in International Banking,* pp. 9–10.

33. Guttentag and Herring, *The Current Crisis in International Lending,* p. 26.

34. Cline, *International Debt: Systemic Risk and Policy Response,* p. 117.

35. Morgan Guaranty Trust Company, *World Financial Markets,* September/October 1985, p. 4.

36. Nicholas D. Kristof, "Quiet Growth of Speciality," *The New York Times,* 17 July 1985, p. D-1.

37. Guttentag and Herring, *The Current Crisis in International Lending,* pp. 17–20.

38. Guttentag and Herring, *The Current Crisis in International Lending,* pp. 11–15.

39. Bergsten, Cline, and Williamson, *Bank Lending to Developing Countries,* pp. 134–138.

40. Jack M. Guttentag and Richard J. Herring, *Commercial Bank Lending to Developing Countries: From Overlending to Underlending to Structural Reform,* Brookings Discussion Papers in International Economics, No. 16, June 1984, p. 32.

41. Bergsten, Cline, and Williamson, *Bank Lending to Developing Countries,* pp. 142–146.

42. For an excellent discussion of these issues, see Henry C. Wallich, *Insuring of Bank Lending to Developing Countries,* Occasional Paper No. 15, Group of Thirty, New York, 1984.

43. Wallich's estimate is based mainly on the experience of American banks prior to the debt crisis. Even as of the third quarter of 1983, however, nonperforming loans for major banks amounted to 3.7 percent of total loans. An insurance facility would presumably apply only to new loans in a bank's portfolio.

44. Bergsten, Cline, and Williamson, *Bank Lending to Developing Countries,* p. 111.

45. Statement of Secretary James Baker before the Annual Meeting of the IMF and World Bank in Seoul, Korea, 8 October 1985.

46. Speech of J. Polak, IMF, executive director, at International Monetary and Trade Conference, Philadelphia, Pa., December 8–10, 1985 (sponsored jointly by the Global Interdependence Center, the Group of Thirty, and the Institute of International Finance). The preponderance of non-U.S. banks extends even to the debt of the ten principal Latin American debtors. Only 35.3 percent of their debt owed to banks in mid-1985 was owed to U.S. banks. Morgan Guaranty Trust Company, *World Financial Markets,* February 1986, Table 3.

47. International bond markets are subdivided into Eurobond and foreign bond markets. Eurobonds are underwritten by an international syndicate and are issued simultaneously in several national markets. Sales are principally in countries other than the country of the currency in which the issue is denominated. Eurobonds are not subject to formal controls. In contrast, foreign bond markets are domestic markets to which foreign borrowers are permitted access. Bonds in these markets are underwritten by a syndicate composed of members from the country in which the sale takes place and are denominated in the currency of that country. Because regulations and entry requirements are much more stringent in foreign bond markets than in the Eurobond market, most developing country bond issues are placed in the Eurobond market.

48. IMF, *International Capital Markets: Developments and Prospects,* Occasional Paper No. 14, 1982, p. 18, and Occasional Paper No. 31, 1984, p. 48 and Table 38.

49. This perception is reflected in the larger-risk premiums paid by developing country borrowers in the foreign bond markets compared with the spread over LIBOR paid by developing countries on international bank loans. David Folkerts-Landau, "The Changing Role of International Bank Lending in Development Finance," *IMF Staff Papers,* June 1985, p. 335.

Memoranda of Comment, Reservation, or Dissent

Harold A. Poling, p. 9

One of the major reasons for U.S. support of the official financing through the World Bank, IMF and IDA is that these institutions can make their lending conditional upon achieving certain policy objectives designed to improve the economic health of the borrowing countries. Unfortunately, the conditions frequently are met in word but not in spirit or deed.

In particular, it is imperative that recipient countries reverse the trend toward government-owned and sponsored enterprises, and take positive steps toward privatizing their government-controlled industrial sectors. The international lending agencies should do three things: first, be more explicit about which type government agencies should be privatized or abolished; second, obtain the agreement of the borrowing country to comply; and third, set up a credible system for monitoring progress. So long as these countries persist in allowing heavily subsidized and inefficient enterprises to absorb the country's resources, the climate for economic growth will be poor.

Roy L. Ash, with which J.W. McSwiney, Ruben F. Mettler, and John Sagan have asked to be associated, p. 21

Quite properly, this statement emphasizes the essential role of a developing nation's own policies in contributing to its growth and discusses a number of specific policy steps a nation should take. Lying behind all such steps is an even more profound, yet often elusive, condition that must first prevail in order for all else to follow.

Positive societal attitudes toward individual freedom, private property and business (including foreign owned) along with a government's reflection of those attitudes in all its works is the sine qua non of effective economic development.

When reasonable degrees of political stability and predictability are added to such underlying societal attitudes, a nation can provide itself the best chance of attracting the factors of production and moving up the growth curve.

Leif H. Olsen, p. 23

Reference is made in several places to capital flight and elsewhere to the importance of creating an economic and political environment conducive to capital inflow. It is important to recognize that the conditions in a country must first and foremost be conducive to discouraging capital flight and encouraging investors who are citizens of that country.

Leif H. Olsen, p. 46

The "absorption" or the "drain" of world savings to the United States oversimplifies what actually occurs and can lead to erroneous conclusions. Many countries consume less than they produce and export the excess, much of it to the United States. The exporter receives dollars for the goods he has sold. He cannot use dollars to pay the costs of producing the goods in the country where the production took place. Thus, he borrows in that country and pays the costs of producing the goods for exportation and instead uses the dollars earned to buy securities in the United States. The exporter's balance sheet shows the loan—tapping the savings of his country—as a liability and the dollar securities as an asset. This entire transaction can and undoubtedly has occurred. But it is most likely that the participants will enter the foreign exchange market to exchange the dollars for the foreign currency needed by the exporter. But buyers of the dollars will by necessity, directly or indirectly—given the fungibility of money borrowed—tap the savings in the exporter's country. Consequently, the savings of countries which export to the United States in actuality are supporting employment, income and capital formation in that country via its exporting economy."

W. Bruce Thomas, p. 47

Only four developing countries entered into VRAs under the President's steel program. Generally, the steel industries concerned are heavily subsidized and the governments entered into the VRAs to avoid penalties under U.S. countervailing duty and antidumping laws.

OBJECTIVES OF THE COMMITTEE FOR ECONOMIC DEVELOPMENT

For over forty years, the Committee for Economic Development has been a respected influence on the formation of business and public policy. CED is devoted to these two objectives:

To develop, through objective research and informed discussion, findings and recommendations for private and public policy that will contribute to preserving and strengthening our free society, achieving steady economic growth at high employment and reasonably stable prices, increasing productivity and living standards, providing greater and more equal opportunity for every citizen, and improving the quality of life for all.

To bring about increasing understanding by present and future leaders in business, government, and education, and among concerned citizens, of the importance of these objectives and the ways in which they can be achieved.

CED's work is supported strictly by private voluntary contributions from business and industry, foundations, and individuals. It is independent, non-profit, nonpartisan, and nonpolitical.

The over 225 trustees, who generally are presidents or board chairmen of corporations and presidents of universities, are chosen for their individual capacities rather than as representatives of any particular interests. By working with scholars, they unite business judgment and experience with scholarship in analyzing the issues and developing recommendations to resolve the economic problems that constantly arise in a dynamic and democratic society.

Through this business-academic partnership, CED endeavors to develop policy statements and other research materials that commend themselves as guides to public and business policy; that can be used as texts in college economics and political science courses and in management training courses; that will be considered and discussed by newspaper and magazine editors, columnists, and commentators; and that are distributed abroad to promote better understanding of the American economic system.

CED believes that by enabling business leaders to demonstrate constructively their concern for the general welfare, it is helping business to earn and maintain the national and community respect essential to the successful functioning of the free enterprise capitalist system.

CED BOARD OF TRUSTEES

CED HONORARY TRUSTEES

RESEARCH ADVISORY BOARD

CED PROFESSIONAL AND ADMINISTRATIVE STAFF

STATEMENTS ON NATIONAL POLICY ISSUED BY THE RESEARCH AND POLICY COMMITTEE

SELECTED PUBLICATIONS

Finance and Third World Economic Growth *(1988)*

Investing in America's Future: Challenges and Opportunities for Public Sector Economic Policies (1988)

Children in Need: Investment Strategies for the Educationally Disadvantaged *(1987)*

Toll of the Twin Deficits *(1987)*

Reforming Health Care: A Market Prescription *(1987)*

Work and Change: Labor Market Adjustment Policies in a Competitive World *(1987)*

Leadership for Dynamic State Economies *(1986)*

Investing in Our Children: Business and the Public Schools *(1985)*

Fighting Federal Deficits: The Time for Hard Choices *(1985)*

Strategy for U.S. Industrial Competitiveness *(1984)*

Strengthening the Federal Budget Process: A Requirement for Effective Fiscal Control *(1983)*

Productivity Policy: Key to the Nation's Economic Future *(1983)*

Energy Prices and Public Policy *(1982)*

Public-Private Partnership: An Opportunity for Urban Communities *(1982)*

Reforming Retirement Policies *(1981)*

Transnational Corporations and Developing Countries: New Policies for a Changing World Economy *(1981)*

Fighting Inflation and Rebuilding a Sound Economy *(1980)*

Stimulating Technological Progress *(1980)*

Helping Insure Our Energy Future: A Program for Developing Synthetic Fuel Plants Now *(1979)*

Redefining Government's Role in the Market System *(1979)*

Improving Management of the Public Work Force: The Challenge to State and Local Government *(1978)*

Jobs for the Hard-to-Employ: New Directions for a Public-Private Partnership *(1978)*

An Approach to Federal Urban Policy *(1977)*

Key Elements of a National Energy Strategy *(1977)*

Nuclear Energy and National Security *(1976)*

Fighting Inflation and Promoting Growth *(1976)*

Improving Productivity in State and Local Government *(1976)*

*International Economic Consequences of High-Priced Energy *(1975)*

Broadcasting and Cable Television:
Policies for Diversity and Change *(1975)*

Achieving Energy Independence *(1974)*

A New U.S. Farm Policy for Changing World Food Needs *(1974)*

Congressional Decision Making for National Security *(1974)*

*Toward a New International Economic System:
A Joint Japanese-American View *(1974)*

More Effective Programs for a Cleaner Environment *(1974)*

The Management and Financing of Colleges *(1973)*

Strengthening the World Monetary System *(1973)*

Financing the Nation's Housing Needs *(1973)*

Building a National Health-Care System *(1973)*

*A New Trade Policy Toward Communist Countries *(1972)*

High Employment Without Inflation:
A Positive Program for Economic Stabilization *(1972)*

Reducing Crime and Assuring Justice *(1972)*

Military Manpower and National Security *(1972)*

The United States and the European Community:
Policies for a Changing World Economy *(1971)*

Social Responsibilities of Business Corporations *(1971)*

Education for the Urban Disadvantaged:
From Preschool to Employment *(1971)*

Further Weapons Against Inflation *(1970)*

Making Congress More Effective *(1970)*

Improving the Public Welfare System *(1970)*

Economic Growth in the United States *(1969)*

Assisting Development in Low-Income Countries *(1969)*

*Nontariff Distortions of Trade *(1969)*

Fiscal and Monetary Policies for Steady Economic Growth *(1969)*

*Trade Policy Toward Low-Income Countries *(1967)*

How Low Income Countries Can Advance Their Own Growth *(1966)*

*Statements issued in association with CED counterpart organizations in foreign countries.

CED COUNTERPART ORGANIZATIONS IN FOREIGN COUNTRIES

Close relations exist between the Committee for Economic Development and independent, nonpolitical research organizations in other countries. Such counterpart groups are composed of business executives and scholars and have objectives similar to those of CED, which they pursue by similarly objective methods. CED cooperates with these organizations on research and study projects of common interest to the various countries concerned. This program has resulted in a number of joint policy statements involving such international matters as energy, East-West trade, assistance to developing countries, and the reduction of nontariff barriers to trade.

CE	Círculo de Empresarios Serrano Jover 5-2° Madrid 8, Spain
CEDA	Committee for Economic Development of Australia 139 Macquarie Street, Sydney 2001, New South Wales, Australia
CEPES	Europäische Vereinigung für Wirtschaftliche und Soziale Entwicklung Reuterweg 14,6000 Frankfurt/Main, West Germany
IDEP	Institut de l'Entreprise 6, rue Clément-Marot, 75008 Paris, France
	Keizai Doyukai (Japan Committee for Economic Development) Japan Industrial Club Bldg. 1 Marunouchi, Chiyoda-ku, Tokyo, Japan
PSI	Policy Studies Institute 100, Park Village East, London NW1 3SR, England
SNS	Studieförbundet Näringsliv och Samhälle Sköldungagatan 2, 11427 Stockholm, Sweden

Index